THE GRINNING GARDENER'S HANDBOOK VOLUME 3

A COMPREHENSIVE GUIDE TO GROWING ORGANIC HERBS FOR CULINARY AND HOLISTIC HEALTH PURPOSES IN DIFFERENT CLIMATES AND SEASONS

KENT JAMESON

Published by:
Kent Jameson Publishing
16394 West Hilton Avenue
Goodyear, AZ 85338
kentjamesonpublishing@gmail.com
Printed in the United States of America.
First Printing, 2024
Library of Congress Cataloging-in-Publication Data:
Kent Jameson
The Grinning Gardener's Handbook Volume 3: A comprehensive guide to growing organic herbs for culinary and holistic health purposes in different climates and seasons.

TABLE OF CONTENTS

INTRODUCTION

"The Grinning Gardener's Handbook Volume 3" aims to be your companion as you explore the joys of growing organic herbs. Whether you seek to enhance your culinary creations or harness the holistic health properties of these plants, this book provides practical, hands-on advice to help you succeed.

This handbook is structured to take you through the process of organic herb gardening, step by step. Building on the insights from previous volumes, it introduces fresh strategies specifically designed for cultivating herbs.

In the first chapter, we'll cover the basics of getting started, including selecting the right herbs for your needs and understanding your local climate. Subsequent chapters will delve into soil health, organic fertilization, pest control, and watering techniques. You'll also find detailed information on planting depth, spacing, and companion planting strategies.

As you progress, we'll explore advanced techniques for maximizing your garden's yield and troubleshooting common issues. We'll discuss the best practices for harvesting and preserving your herbs to ensure they retain their flavor and potency. Additionally, there will be chapters dedicated to using your herbs in culinary recipes and for holistic health purposes, from teas to tinctures.

My commitment to organic gardening is reflected in every page of this book. I have seen firsthand the benefits of working in harmony with nature, and I am passionate about sharing that knowledge with you.

This book is for anyone who wants to grow herbs for culinary or holistic purposes. It caters to both beginners and experienced gardeners looking to expand their knowledge. Whether you have a sprawling garden or a small balcony, you will find valuable insights and practical tips to help you succeed.

By the end of this book, you will have the knowledge and confidence to grow, harvest, and use a variety of herbs. You will understand how to create a thriving garden that suits your climate and needs. More importantly, you will experience the satisfaction and joy that comes from cultivating your own herbs.

I encourage you to actively engage with this journey. Keep a gardening journal to document your progress and experiments. Try different herbs and techniques to see what works best for you. Share your experiences with the gardening community and learn from others along the way.

Gardening is more than just a hobby; it is a way of life. It connects us to the earth, to our food, and to each other. As you embark on this journey, embrace the process and take pleasure in each step. There will be challenges, but the rewards are immeasurable. Your garden will not only provide you with fresh, flavorful herbs but also with a sense of accomplishment and peace.

Welcome to the world of organic herb gardening. Let's get started, and may your garden be bountiful and your journey fulfilling.

CHAPTER 1

GETTING STARTED WITH ORGANIC HERB GARDENING

1.1 UNDERSTANDING ORGANIC GARDENING PRINCIPLES

Organic gardening is more than just avoiding synthetic chemicals; it's about working with nature to create a healthy, sustainable growing environment. At its core, organic gardening relies on natural methods to nourish the soil and manage pests. This approach not only benefits your garden but also supports the broader ecosystem. By enriching the soil with compost and natural fertilizers, you create a thriving environment for your herbs. These practices foster a rich biodiversity, attracting beneficial insects and microorganisms that help keep your garden balanced. The avoidance of synthetic chemicals ensures that your garden remains a haven for pollinators like bees and butterflies, which are crucial for the health of your plants.

The philosophy behind organic gardening is rooted in sustainability and environmental stewardship. This holistic approach emphasizes the importance of creating a self-sustaining ecosystem that mimics natural cycles. By focusing on building healthy soil and using natural resources responsibly, you contribute to a more sustainable world. Organic gardening promotes the idea that we are caretakers of the earth, and our actions should reflect a commitment to preserving natural resources for future generations. This means using water wisely, recycling organic waste into compost, and choosing plants that are well-suited to your local climate and conditions.

Permaculture is a concept that can seamlessly integrate into your organic herb gardening practices. Inspired by natural ecosystems, permaculture design principles aim to create sustainable and self-sufficient growing systems. One key aspect of permaculture is companion planting, where different plants are grown together to support each other's growth. For example, planting basil alongside tomatoes can help repel pests and improve the flavor of the tomatoes. Polyculture, another permaculture principle, involves cultivating a diverse mix of plants in the same space, which can enhance soil health and reduce the risk of disease. By adopting these techniques, you can create a resilient and productive herb garden that works in harmony with nature.

Maintaining and improving soil health is a cornerstone of organic gardening. Healthy soil is teeming with life, from earthworms and beneficial insects to a myriad of microorganisms that break down organic matter and release nutrients. Composting is an excellent way to enrich your soil with organic matter. By recycling kitchen scraps, yard waste, and other organic materials into compost, you create a nutrient-rich amendment that improves soil structure and fertility. Green manure, such as cover crops, can also be used to add nutrients to the soil. These plants are grown specifically to be turned back into the soil, where they decompose and release valuable nutrients. Mulching is another effective technique for maintaining soil health. By covering the soil with a layer of organic material, such as straw or leaves, you help retain moisture, suppress weeds, and reduce soil erosion.

As you embark on your organic herb gardening journey, keep these principles in mind. By working with nature and adopting sustainable practices, you will not only create a thriving herb garden but also contribute to the health of the planet. The benefits of organic gardening extend beyond your garden; they foster a deeper connection to the natural world and a sense of responsibility for its well-being. Whether you have a small windowsill garden or a larger plot, these principles will guide you in creating a productive and sustainable herb garden that brings joy and nourishment to your life.

1.2 CHOOSING THE RIGHT HERBS FOR BEGINNERS

Selecting the right herbs to start with is crucial for a successful and satisfying gardening experience. For beginners, it's best to opt for herbs that are easy to grow, hardy, and versatile in their uses. The following list includes four beginner-friendly herbs that are perfect for those just starting their gardening adventure: basil, mint, parsley, and chives. Each of these herbs has unique growing conditions and offers a range of culinary and holistic health benefits, ensuring you get the most out of your herb garden.

Basil

Basil is a beloved herb known for its sweet, aromatic leaves that are a staple in many cuisines. It thrives in full sun, requiring at least six hours of direct sunlight daily. Basil prefers well-drained soil that's kept consistently moist but not waterlogged. This herb is sensitive to cold, so it's best to plant it after the last frost date in your area. In the kitchen, basil shines in pesto, adding a burst of flavor to pasta and salads. It also makes a soothing tea that can help alleviate stress and digestive issues. Basil contains essential oils that have anti-inflammatory and antibacterial properties, making it a valuable addition to your holistic health herb collection.

Mint

Mint is another excellent choice for beginners, known for its refreshing scent and vigorous growth. Mint can tolerate partial shade but flourishes in full sun. It prefers moist, well-drained soil and should be watered regularly to maintain its lush foliage. Mint can be quite invasive, so it's wise to plant it in containers to prevent it from overtaking your garden. This versatile herb is perfect for making refreshing drinks like mojitos and iced teas, as well as adding a cool flavor to desserts and savory dishes. Holistically, mint is renowned for its digestive benefits, helping to soothe upset stomachs and relieve indigestion. Its menthol content also provides a natural remedy for headaches and respiratory issues.

Parsley

Parsley is a biennial herb often used as a garnish but offers much more in terms of flavor and nutrition. It grows well in full sun to partial shade and prefers rich, well-drained soil. Parsley needs regular watering, especially during dry spells, to keep its leaves vibrant and lush. This herb is a fantastic addition to salads, soups, and sauces, providing a fresh, slightly peppery taste. Parsley's high vitamin C content and anti-inflammatory properties make it a wonderful holistic health herb, aiding in immune support and reducing inflammation. It can also help freshen breath, making it a natural choice for oral health.

Chives

Chives are a hardy perennial herb that is easy to grow and maintain. They thrive in full sun but can tolerate light shade. Chives prefer well-drained soil with consistent moisture. Once established, they require minimal care and will return year after year. The mild onion flavor of chives makes them perfect for sprinkling over baked potatoes, omelets, and salads. Chives also have holistic benefits, including antibacterial properties that can help fight infections and support digestive health. The beautiful purple flowers of chives are edible and add a decorative touch to dishes.

When it comes to sourcing quality seeds or plants, there are several reliable options. Local nurseries often carry a wide selection of herb plants that are well-suited to your region's climate. Shopping at a local nursery allows you to see the plants in person and get advice from knowledgeable staff. Online seed companies are another excellent resource, offering a vast array of herb seeds that you can browse from the comfort of your home. Look for reputable companies with good reviews and a commitment to organic practices. Heirloom seed providers are also worth considering, as they offer seeds that have been passed down through generations, preserving the genetic diversity and unique flavors of traditional herb varieties.

Starting with these beginner-friendly herbs will set you on the path to a thriving herb garden. By understanding their growing conditions and taking advantage of their culinary and holistic uses, you'll be well-equipped to enjoy the many benefits of herb gardening. Whether you're growing them in a small windowsill garden or a larger outdoor space, these herbs are sure to bring flavor, health, and beauty into your life.

1.3 SETTING UP YOUR GARDENING SPACE: FROM WINDOWSILLS TO BACKYARDS

Finding the right space for your herb garden is crucial. Whether you're limited to a small windowsill or have access to a sprawling backyard, there's a way to make it work. For those with limited indoor space, windowsills offer a practical solution. An east or south-facing window can provide the six hours of sunlight most herbs need. Arrange your pots in a single row to ensure each plant gets adequate light. If you're using small pots, place them on trays to catch excess water and prevent damage to your windowsill. It's also wise to rotate the pots occasionally, ensuring even growth as they reach for the light.

Balconies and patios offer a bit more space and flexibility. Here, you can experiment with container gardening and vertical gardening solutions. Hanging baskets are excellent for herbs that trail, like oregano and thyme, while tall pots are perfect for herbs with deep roots, such as rosemary. If you're short on floor space, consider using wall-mounted planters or vertical garden structures. These not only save space but also create an attractive, green wall that can enhance your outdoor living area. Arrange your containers so that taller plants don't overshadow smaller ones, ensuring even sunlight distribution.

Raised garden beds and traditional garden plots provide ample space for more extensive herb gardens. Raised beds are particularly beneficial for those who want better control over soil quality and drainage. They can be built to any height, making them accessible for gardeners who prefer not to bend down. Traditional garden plots offer the freedom to plant a variety of herbs in a more natural setting. In both cases, plan your layout carefully. Group herbs with similar water and sunlight needs together. Use taller plants as natural windbreaks for more delicate herbs. Companion planting can also be employed to enhance growth and deter pests.

Sunlight and air circulation are vital for healthy herb growth. Herbs generally need a minimum of six hours of direct sunlight each day. Without adequate light, herbs become leggy and weak.

Air circulation is equally important as it helps prevent mold and mildew, which can devastate your plants. Make sure your garden space has good airflow. Indoors, this might mean keeping a small fan nearby to keep the air moving. Outdoors, avoid overcrowding plants and ensure there's enough space for air to circulate freely around each one.

Preparing your chosen gardening space involves a few key steps. Start by cleaning and organizing the area. Remove any debris or old plant material that could harbor pests or diseases. If you're using containers, ensure they have proper drainage holes. Line the bottom with a layer of gravel or broken pottery pieces to improve drainage further. For raised beds, fill them with a high-quality soil mix that's rich in organic matter. If you're working with a traditional garden plot, test your soil and amend it as necessary. Adding compost or well-rotted manure can significantly improve soil fertility and structure.

Once your space is clean and organized, it's time to set up your containers or beds. Arrange them in a layout that maximizes sunlight exposure. Place taller containers or raised beds in the back and shorter ones in the front. This ensures that all your herbs receive adequate light. If you're using a garden plot, plan your rows so they run north to south, allowing for even sunlight distribution throughout the day.

Proper drainage is crucial for preventing root rot and other water-related issues. Ensure your containers have drainage holes and use a well-draining soil mix. For raised beds and garden plots, consider adding organic matter like compost to improve soil structure and drainage. Mulching around your herbs can also help retain moisture while preventing weeds.

Setting up your gardening space might seem daunting at first, but with careful planning, you can create a thriving herb garden in any environment. Whether you're working with a tiny windowsill or a spacious backyard, the principles remain the same. Prioritize sunlight and air circulation, prepare your soil well, and choose the right containers or beds for your space. With these steps, you'll be well on your way to enjoying the many benefits of growing your own herbs.

1.4 ESSENTIAL TOOLS AND SUPPLIES FOR HERB GARDENING

Having the right tools and supplies can make all the difference in your gardening experience. These tools not only help you work more efficiently but also ensure that your plants receive the care they need to thrive.

Hand Trowel

One of the most fundamental tools in any gardener's arsenal is the hand trowel. This small, sturdy tool is perfect for digging small holes, transplanting seedlings, and even removing weeds. When selecting a hand trowel, look for one with a comfortable grip and a strong, rust-resistant blade. Stainless steel trowels are durable and easy to clean, making them a worthwhile investment.

Pruning Shears

Pruning shears are another must-have tool for any herb gardener. These are essential for trimming herbs, removing dead or diseased foliage, and shaping plants to encourage healthy growth. There are two main types of pruning shears: bypass and anvil. Bypass pruners work like scissors, making clean cuts and are ideal for live, green stems. Anvil pruners, on the other hand, have a single sharp blade that cuts against a flat surface and are better suited for dead or woody stems. Regularly sharpen your pruning shears to maintain their cutting efficiency. A sharp blade makes cleaner cuts, which helps prevent plant damage and disease entry.

Watering Can

A watering can or hose with a gentle spray nozzle is crucial for keeping your herbs hydrated. Herbs typically prefer a steady, even watering that mimics natural rainfall. A watering can with a rose attachment disperses water gently, reducing the risk of washing away soil or damaging delicate seedlings. For larger gardens, a hose with an adjustable spray nozzle allows you to control the water flow and pressure, ensuring that each plant gets the right amount of moisture. After each use, empty any remaining water from your watering can to prevent rust and bacteria buildup. Store hoses coiled neatly to avoid kinks and prolong their lifespan.

Gloves

Garden gloves are indispensable for protecting your hands from thorns, splinters, and soilborne pathogens. A good pair of gloves will fit snugly without being too tight, allowing for dexterity while shielding your skin. Look for gloves made from breathable, water-resistant materials that can withstand wear and tear. Gloves with reinforced fingertips and padded palms offer extra protection and comfort during heavy tasks like digging or pruning. After gardening, wash your gloves to remove dirt and debris and let them air dry to maintain their condition.

Maintaining your tools is as important as having the right ones. Clean your tools after each use to remove soil and plant residue, which can harbor pests and diseases. For tools with blades, like pruning shears, a quick wipe down with a cloth and some rubbing alcohol helps prevent rust and keeps them sanitary. Sharpen blades regularly using a whetstone or a sharpening tool to ensure they remain effective. Store your tools in a dry, sheltered place, such as a garden shed or garage, to protect them from the elements and extend their lifespan.

In addition to tools, certain supplies are vital for organic herb gardening. Organic fertilizers, like compost and compost tea, provide essential nutrients to your plants. Compost is rich in organic matter, improving soil structure and fertility. It's easy to make at home using kitchen scraps, yard waste, and other organic materials.

Compost tea, a liquid extract of compost, can be used as a foliar spray or soil drench to boost plant health. Organic mulch options, such as straw, leaves, or wood chips, help retain moisture, suppress weeds, and regulate soil temperature. Applying a layer of mulch around your herbs can significantly improve their growing conditions.

Natural pest repellents, like neem oil, are essential for managing pests without resorting to synthetic chemicals. Neem oil is derived from the seeds of the neem tree and is effective against a wide range of insect pests. It works by disrupting the life cycle of insects, preventing them from feeding, molting, or reproducing. Spray neem oil on your plants every couple of weeks as a preventative measure and more frequently if you notice signs of pest activity.

When it comes to sourcing quality tools and supplies, there are several options to consider. Local garden centers are a great place to start. They often carry a wide range of tools and supplies, and the staff can provide valuable advice tailored to your local growing conditions. Online retailers offer a vast selection and the convenience of home delivery. Look for reputable sellers with positive reviews to ensure you receive high-quality products. Community gardening groups and swaps are also excellent resources. These events allow you to purchase or trade tools and supplies with fellow gardeners, often at a lower cost than retail stores.

Equipped with the right tools and supplies, you'll be well-prepared to care for your herb garden effectively. From the precision of pruning shears to the nourishment provided by organic fertilizers, each tool and supply plays a crucial role in your gardening success. Maintaining your tools ensures they remain effective, while sourcing quality supplies supports the health and productivity of your plants. Whether you're digging, pruning, watering, or protecting your herbs, having the proper equipment will make your gardening experience more enjoyable and rewarding.

As you begin your journey into organic herb gardening, remember that the right tools and supplies are your allies. They make the tasks of planting, nurturing, and harvesting more manageable, allowing you to focus on the joy and satisfaction that comes from growing your own herbs. With careful selection and maintenance of your tools, combined with the use of organic fertilizers and pest control solutions, you'll create a thriving herb garden that provides fresh, flavorful, and healthy herbs for all your culinary and holistic health needs.

CHAPTER 2
PREPARING YOUR SOIL
AND PLANTING

This chapter will guide you through the essential steps of
assessing and improving your soil, ensuring a strong foundation for your herb garden.

2.1 ASSESSING AND IMPROVING SOIL QUALITY

Understanding the quality of your soil is crucial for successful herb gardening. The first step in this process is performing a soil test to determine its pH and nutrient levels. Soil pH indicates how acidic or basic your soil is, which affects the availability of nutrients to your plants. Nutrient levels, on the other hand, provide insight into the presence of essential elements like nitrogen, phosphorus, and potassium.

To perform a basic soil test, you have two main options: DIY soil test kits or sending samples to a local extension office. DIY soil test kits are readily available at garden centers and are easy to use. They typically include pH test strips or capsules and instructions on how to collect and test your soil. While convenient, these kits may not be as accurate as professional testing. If you seek a more comprehensive analysis, consider sending soil samples to a local extension office. These offices offer detailed testing services that include pH, nutrient levels, and recommendations for soil amendments based on your results. For collecting soil samples, dig about 6 to 8 inches deep, removing any roots, grass, or mulch. Mix soil from different areas of your garden to get a representative sample.

Recognizing the type of soil you have is another important aspect of soil assessment. There are three main types of soil: sandy, clay, and loamy.

Sandy soil is known for its good drainage but poor nutrient retention. It feels gritty and falls apart easily when wet. While sandy soil allows water to flow through quickly, it also means that nutrients can leach away, making it less fertile.

Clay soil, on the other hand, has high nutrient content but poor drainage. It feels sticky when wet and forms hard clumps when dry. This type of soil can hold onto water and nutrients well but can become waterlogged and compacted, making it difficult for roots to penetrate.

Loamy soil is considered the ideal soil type for gardening. It has a balanced mixture of sand, silt, and clay, providing good drainage, nutrient retention, and aeration. Loamy soil feels crumbly and moist, making it easy to work with and highly fertile.

Improving soil structure is vital for creating a healthy growing environment for your herbs. One of the most effective ways to enhance soil health is by adding organic matter. Compost is an excellent source of organic matter, enriching the soil with nutrients and improving its texture. You can make your own compost using kitchen scraps, yard waste, and other organic materials. Incorporating aged manure into your soil is another effective method. Manure adds essential nutrients like nitrogen, phosphorus, and potassium, which are crucial for plant growth. Be sure to use well-aged manure to avoid burning your plants with excess nitrogen. Cover crops, such as clover or legumes, are another valuable addition to your soil improvement toolkit. These plants are grown specifically to be turned back into the soil, adding nitrogen and organic matter as they decompose.

The role of microorganisms in soil health cannot be overstated. Beneficial bacteria and fungi, along with earthworms and other decomposers, play a crucial role in breaking down organic matter and releasing nutrients. These microorganisms create a thriving soil ecosystem that supports plant growth. To foster a healthy soil ecosystem, avoid using synthetic chemicals that can harm beneficial organisms. Instead, focus on organic practices that encourage biodiversity. Adding compost and organic matter regularly provides food for microorganisms, helping them thrive. Mulching your garden beds helps retain moisture and provides a habitat for earthworms and other beneficial creatures.

By assessing and improving your soil, you lay the groundwork for a successful herb garden. Understanding your soil's pH, nutrient levels, and structure allows you to make informed decisions that enhance soil health and fertility. Incorporating organic matter and fostering a thriving soil ecosystem ensures that your herbs have the best possible environment to grow and flourish. This foundational work sets the stage for a productive and rewarding gardening experience.

2.2 ORGANIC SOIL AMENDMENTS AND FERTILIZERS

As you prepare to cultivate a thriving herb garden, understanding the role of organic soil amendments is crucial. These natural materials improve soil structure, enhance fertility, and support the overall health of your plants. Compost is one of the most versatile and beneficial amendments you can add to your soil. It enriches the soil with essential nutrients and organic matter, improving its texture and water-holding capacity. To create your own compost, start by building a compost bin in a convenient location. Balance green materials like vegetable scraps and grass clippings with brown materials such as leaves and straw. Turn the compost regularly to aerate it, which speeds up the decomposition process. Once the compost is dark, crumbly, and has an earthy smell, it's ready to use. Spread a layer of compost over your garden beds or mix it into the soil to give your herbs a nutrient boost.

Aged manure is another excellent organic amendment. It adds essential nutrients like nitrogen, phosphorus, and potassium, which are vital for plant growth. Unlike fresh manure, aged manure has decomposed to a point where it won't burn your plants. It's best to incorporate aged manure into the soil before planting. This allows the nutrients to integrate well with the soil and become readily available to your plants. Leaf mold, made from decomposed leaves, is particularly beneficial for enhancing soil structure and moisture retention. Collect fallen leaves, pile them up in a corner of your garden, and let them decompose over several months. Once the leaves have broken down into a dark, crumbly texture, you can use leaf mold as mulch or mix it into the soil to improve its quality.

In addition to these amendments, natural fertilizers play a significant role in maintaining soil fertility. Fish emulsion is a liquid fertilizer made from decomposed fish parts. It's rich in nitrogen and provides a quick nutrient boost to your plants. Apply fish emulsion by diluting it with water according to the instructions and watering your plants with the solution. This is particularly useful during the early stages of plant growth when herbs need a lot of nitrogen. Bone meal, another natural fertilizer, is a great source of phosphorus, which promotes strong root development. Sprinkle bone meal into the planting holes or mix it into the soil before sowing seeds or transplanting seedlings. Seaweed extract is packed with trace minerals and growth hormones that support overall plant health. Use it as a foliar spray or soil drench to provide your herbs with an extra dose of nutrients.

Timing and method of application are critical when using soil amendments and fertilizers. Before planting, prepare your soil by incorporating organic matter like compost and aged manure. This creates a nutrient-rich environment for your herbs to thrive in. Throughout the growing season, monitor your plants and apply mid-season nutrient boosts as needed. For example, if your herbs show signs of nutrient deficiency, such as yellowing leaves or stunted growth, a dose of fish emulsion or seaweed extract can help. After harvesting, rejuvenate your soil by adding more compost or aged manure. This replenishes the nutrients that your plants have used up and prepares the soil for the next planting cycle.

Understanding and utilizing organic soil amendments and fertilizers will set the stage for a healthy and productive herb garden.
By enriching your soil with these natural materials, you create an
optimal growing environment for your plants. This not only
enhances the quality and yield of your herbs but also supports
long-term soil health and sustainability. With these practices,
you'll be well-equipped to nurture a vibrant and bountiful herb
garden.

2.3 SEED STARTING VS. TRANSPLANTS: WHICH IS RIGHT FOR YOU?

When deciding whether to start your herbs from seeds or buy
transplants, consider both the benefits and drawbacks. Starting
from seeds is cost-effective and offers a wider variety of herb
options. You gain control over every stage of growth, allowing you
to nurture your plants from the very beginning. However, starting
seeds requires patience and dedication. You'll need to provide the
right conditions for germination and growth, which can be time-
consuming.

On the other hand, transplants offer the convenience of a head
start. By purchasing young plants, you skip the germination phase
and get an immediate, tangible result. This method is particularly
useful if you want a quicker harvest or if you're new to gardening
and want to avoid the complexities of seed starting. The downside
is that transplants are generally more expensive than seeds and
offer fewer varieties. Additionally, transplanted herbs may experience shock, slowing their growth initially.

Starting Seeds Indoors: A Step-by-Step Guide

To start seeds indoors successfully, begin by choosing the right
seed-starting medium. Opt for a light, well-draining mix specifi-

cally designed for seed starting. Avoid regular garden soil, which can be too heavy and may contain pathogens. Fill your seed trays or pots with the medium, leaving a small gap at the top. Moisten the soil before planting the seeds, ensuring it's damp but not waterlogged.

Proper lighting and temperature are crucial for seed germination. Place your seed trays in a warm, bright location, ideally with temperatures between 65-75°F. If natural light is insufficient, use grow lights to provide the necessary light spectrum. Position the lights just a few inches above the seedlings and adjust them as the plants grow. Aim for 12-16 hours of light per day to support healthy growth.

Maintaining the right level of moisture is also important. Use a spray bottle to mist the soil surface, keeping it consistently moist but not soggy. Cover the seed trays with a plastic lid or wrap them in a plastic bag to create a humid environment. Once the seedlings emerge, remove the cover to prevent damping-off disease, a common issue that causes seedlings to collapse and die.

Before transplanting your seedlings outdoors, they need to be hardened off. This process gradually acclimates the young plants to outdoor conditions. Start by placing the seedlings in a sheltered, shady spot for a few hours each day, gradually increasing their exposure to sunlight and outdoor temperatures over the course of a week or two. This helps reduce transplant shock and prepares the seedlings for the harsher outdoor environment.

Transplanting Young Plants: Best Practices

When transplanting young plants, preparation is key. Begin by selecting a suitable planting site that offers the right conditions for your herbs, including adequate sunlight and well-draining soil.

Dig holes that are slightly larger than the root balls of your seedlings, spacing them according to the specific needs of each herb. For example, basil plants should be spaced 12-18 inches apart, while chives need about 8-12 inches of space.

Gently remove the seedlings from their containers, taking care not to damage the roots. If the roots are tightly bound, gently tease them apart to encourage better growth. Place the seedlings into the prepared holes, ensuring they are planted at the same depth they were growing in their containers. Fill in the holes with soil, firming it gently around the plants to eliminate air pockets.

Water the transplants thoroughly after planting to help settle the soil and establish good root-to-soil contact. Mulch around the base of the plants to retain moisture, suppress weeds, and regulate soil temperature. Keep an eye on the newly transplanted herbs, watering them regularly until they become established.

Common Issues and Solutions for Both Methods

Both seed starting and transplanting can present challenges, but with a little knowledge, you can overcome them. One common issue when starting seeds is damping-off disease, which causes seedlings to wilt and die. To prevent this, ensure good air circulation around the seedlings and avoid overwatering. Using a sterile seed-starting mix and clean containers can also reduce the risk of this disease.

Transplant shock is a common problem when moving young plants to the garden. To minimize shock, harden off the seedlings properly and transplant them on a cloudy day or in the late afternoon to reduce stress from the sun. Water the transplants well and provide temporary shade if necessary.

Pests and diseases can affect both seedlings and transplants. Keep an eye out for common pests like aphids, which can be controlled with insecticidal soap or neem oil. Fungal diseases can be managed by ensuring good air circulation and avoiding overhead watering. Regularly inspect your plants for signs of trouble and act quickly to address any issues.

Whether you choose to start from seeds or use transplants, understanding the benefits and challenges of each method will help you make informed decisions. By providing the right conditions and care, you can enjoy a thriving herb garden that provides fresh, flavorful, and medicinally beneficial herbs.

2.4 PLANTING DEPTH, SPACING, AND COMPANION PLANTING

Understanding the correct planting depth for various herbs is fundamental for ensuring successful germination and growth. Basil seeds, for instance, require shallow planting; just a light covering of soil is enough. This allows them to receive the warmth and light they need to sprout. Mint, on the other hand, should be planted slightly deeper to accommodate its spreading root system. Covering mint seeds with about a quarter inch of soil helps them establish a strong root base. Parsley seeds also benefit from being planted at a depth of about a quarter inch. This depth provides the right conditions for optimal germination and growth. Each herb has specific requirements, and knowing these can make a significant difference in your gardening success.

Proper plant spacing is equally important for healthy herb growth. Basil plants, for example, should be spaced 12 to 18 inches apart. This spacing allows for adequate air circulation, reducing the risk of fungal diseases and ensuring that each plant has enough room to grow. Chives, being smaller, can be planted closer together, with 8 to 12 inches of space between each plant. This closer spacing helps them form a dense, attractive clump. Rosemary, a larger and more robust herb, needs more room to spread out. Planting rosemary 24 to 36 inches apart ensures that it receives sufficient sunlight and airflow, promoting healthy growth and reducing the likelihood of pest infestations. By understanding and implementing proper spacing, you create an environment where each herb can thrive.

Companion planting is a powerful technique that leverages the natural relationships between plants to enhance growth and deter pests. Pairing basil with tomatoes, for example, not only enhances the flavor of the tomatoes but also helps repel pests like aphids and whiteflies. The strong scent of basil confuses these pests, making it harder for them to locate the tomatoes. Mint, known for its vigorous growth and strong aroma, can be planted near cabbage to deter cabbage moths. The scent of mint masks the smell of cabbage, making it less attractive to the moths. Parsley, with its ability to attract beneficial insects like ladybugs and hoverflies, can be planted near carrots. These insects prey on common garden pests, providing natural pest control and improving the health and productivity of both plants.

Implementing companion planting in your garden involves a bit of planning and creativity. Creating polycultures, or mixed plantings, can mimic natural ecosystems and promote a diverse and resilient garden environment. For example, planting a mixture of herbs, flowers, and vegetables in the same bed can reduce pest problems and improve overall plant health. Rotating crops each season helps maintain soil health by preventing the buildup of pests and diseases that target specific plants. For instance, if you plant basil in one spot this year, consider planting a different herb or vegetable in that spot next year. This rotation disrupts the life cycles of pests and reduces the likelihood of soil depletion.

Using herbs as natural pest repellents is another practical tip for companion planting. Herbs like marigold and nasturtium can be interplanted with your herbs to repel a variety of pests. Marigolds, for example, release compounds that deter nematodes, while nasturtiums attract aphids away from your main crops. By strategically placing these companion plants, you can create a more balanced and harmonious garden ecosystem that relies less on chemical interventions.

With these strategies in place, your garden will not only be more productive but also more resilient to pests and diseases. Proper planting depth and spacing, combined with the principles of companion planting, set the stage for a healthy and thriving herb garden. These practices foster a balanced ecosystem where plants support each other, leading to better yields and a more enjoyable gardening experience.

As you prepare to plant your herbs, remember that these foundational practices are key to your success. The next chapter will delve into watering techniques and soil health management, ensuring your herbs receive the right care throughout their growth.

CHAPTER 3
WATERING TECHNIQUES AND SOIL HEALTH MANAGEMENT

I n this chapter, we'll explore the nuances of watering different herbs and how to keep your garden thriving, even in challenging climates.

3.1 UNDERSTANDING WATERING NEEDS FOR DIFFERENT HERBS

Each herb has its own specific watering requirements, and understanding these needs is essential for their healthy growth. Basil, for example, thrives in evenly moist soil. It doesn't tolerate drought well, so it's important to water it regularly, ensuring the soil remains consistently damp but not waterlogged. During the hot summer months, basil may need more frequent watering to prevent the soil from drying out. On the other hand, rosemary is quite different. This hardy herb is native to the Mediterranean, where it grows in sandy, well-drained soils. Rosemary prefers drier conditions and can tolerate periods of drought. Overwatering rosemary can lead to root rot, so it's best to let the soil dry out between waterings.

Mint is another herb with unique watering needs. It requires consistently moist soil to thrive. Mint's vigorous growth and spreading habit mean it drinks up water quickly, especially during warm weather. Keeping the soil evenly moist, but not saturated, helps mint maintain its lush, green foliage. Thyme, in contrast, thrives in well-drained soil and needs less frequent watering. This herb is drought-tolerant and does well in sandy or rocky soils. Overwatering thyme can cause its roots to rot, so it's crucial to let the soil dry out between waterings. Understanding these individual needs is key to ensuring each herb in your garden flourishes.

Climate plays a significant role in determining your garden's watering needs. In hot and dry climates, herbs may require increased watering frequency to prevent soil from drying out too quickly. The intense sun and high temperatures can cause soil to lose moisture rapidly, making it essential to monitor your plants closely. Herbs like basil and mint, which prefer consistently moist soil, may need daily watering during the peak of summer.

Conversely, in humid climates, the risk of overwatering increases. High humidity levels can cause the soil to retain moisture longer, which can lead to root rot in herbs like rosemary and thyme that prefer drier conditions. It's important to adjust your watering schedule to account for the increased moisture in the air and soil.

In cooler climates, the watering needs of your herbs will generally be reduced during the colder months. As temperatures drop, plant growth slows, and the soil retains moisture longer. Herbs like rosemary and thyme, which are more drought-tolerant, may only need occasional watering during this time. However, be mindful of indoor herb gardens during winter, as indoor heating can dry out the air and soil, necessitating more frequent watering. Always check the soil moisture before watering to avoid overwatering.

Monitoring soil moisture levels is crucial for meeting your herbs' hydration needs accurately. One simple method is the finger test. Insert your finger about an inch into the soil. If it feels dry, it's time to water. This quick and easy test helps you gauge the moisture content in the top layer of soil, where most herb roots are located. For a more precise measurement, consider using a moisture meter. These tools provide an accurate reading of soil moisture, helping you determine when to water your plants. They are particularly useful for beginners who are still learning to judge soil moisture by feel.

Visual cues are also helpful in assessing your herbs' watering needs. Wilting leaves are a common sign of underwatering. If your herbs look droopy and the soil feels dry, they likely need a good drink. Conversely, yellowing leaves can indicate overwatering. If the soil is consistently wet and the leaves are turning yellow, it's a sign that your plants are receiving too much water, potentially leading to root rot. Adjust your watering accordingly to correct these issues. Additionally, observing the overall appearance and soil condition can provide valuable insights. Dry, crumbly soil and plants with dry, wilting leaves signal a need for more frequent watering. On the other hand, soggy soil and yellowing leaves indicate overwatering and the need to reduce watering frequency.

Recognizing and correcting watering issues is essential for maintaining a healthy herb garden. Overwatering is a common problem that can lead to yellowing leaves and root rot. When the roots are constantly submerged in water, they can't access the oxygen they need, leading to decay. To prevent this, ensure your pots and garden beds have proper drainage and avoid watering until the soil has dried out. Underwatering, on the other hand, causes wilting and dry, crumbly soil. If your herbs are drooping and the soil is dry, increase your watering frequency. Providing the right amount of water is a delicate balance, but with careful observation and adjustments, you can keep your herbs thriving.

As you nurture your herb garden, remember that each plant has unique needs. By understanding these requirements and tailoring your watering practices to suit your local climate, you'll create an environment where your herbs can flourish. Monitoring soil moisture levels and recognizing the signs of overwatering and underwatering will help you maintain a healthy, productive garden. This foundation of proper watering techniques sets the stage for a thriving herb garden, full of vibrant, flavorful plants.

3.2 TECHNIQUES FOR EFFICIENT AND EFFECTIVE WATERING

Watering your herbs efficiently and effectively can make a significant difference in their health and productivity. There are several methods to consider, each with its own advantages. Hand watering is a versatile and straightforward approach, using either a watering can or a hose. This method allows you to control the amount of water each plant receives, making it ideal for small gardens or potted herbs. When hand watering, aim the water at the base of the plants rather than the leaves to minimize the risk of fungal diseases.

For larger gardens or those looking for a more automated solution, drip irrigation is an excellent choice. This system delivers water slowly and steadily directly to the root zone of the plants through a network of tubes and emitters. Drip irrigation conserves water by reducing evaporation and runoff, ensuring that every drop goes where it's needed most. It also helps prevent the foliage from getting wet, which can reduce the risk of fungal infections. Soaker hoses work on a similar principle, distributing water evenly along their length. They are laid out on the soil surface and deliver water directly to the root zone, making them ideal for garden beds and rows of herbs.

Overhead sprinklers are another option, providing broad coverage for larger areas. While they are convenient for watering a large garden quickly, they come with some drawbacks. Overhead sprinklers can wet the foliage, increasing the risk of fungal diseases, and they are less efficient than drip irrigation or soaker hoses due to higher evaporation rates. If you choose to use overhead sprinklers, do so early in the morning to allow the foliage to dry quickly and minimize disease risk.

The benefits of drip irrigation and soaker hoses are numerous. These methods are highly efficient, using water more effectively and reducing waste. By delivering water directly to the root zone, they minimize evaporation and runoff, making them ideal for water conservation. This targeted approach also helps prevent the foliage from getting wet, reducing the risk of fungal diseases. Additionally, these systems can be automated with timers, ensuring your herbs receive consistent watering even when you're not around.

Watering at the right time of day is crucial for maximizing efficiency and minimizing disease risk. Early morning is the best time to water your herbs. The cooler temperatures reduce evaporation, allowing the water to penetrate the soil more effectively. Additionally, watering in the morning gives the foliage time to dry throughout the day, reducing the risk of fungal diseases. Evening watering, while sometimes convenient, can leave the foliage damp overnight, creating an ideal environment for fungal growth. If you must water in the evening, try to water the soil directly and avoid wetting the leaves.

Creating a consistent watering schedule is essential for maintaining healthy herbs. The frequency of watering depends on the type of herb and the climate you're in. For instance, herbs like basil and mint, which prefer consistently moist soil, may need watering every day during hot, dry weather. In contrast, rosemary and thyme, which tolerate drier conditions, can go longer between waterings. Start by observing your plants and their needs, then adjust your schedule accordingly. Seasonal changes also affect watering needs. During the hot summer months, you may need to water more frequently, while in cooler, wetter seasons, you can reduce the frequency.

Monitoring and tweaking your watering schedule as needed is key to ensuring your herbs receive the right amount of water. Use tools like moisture meters for precise measurements and keep an eye on the weather forecast to adjust your watering accordingly. For instance, if rain is expected, you can skip a scheduled watering. Regularly check the soil moisture and the condition of your plants to ensure they are getting the water they need without being overwatered.

By employing these efficient and effective watering techniques, you can ensure your herbs receive the optimal amount of water, promoting healthy growth and productivity. Whether you choose hand watering, drip irrigation, or soaker hoses, understanding the benefits and best practices of each method will help you create a thriving herb garden.

3.3 MULCHING AND ITS BENEFITS FOR SOIL HEALTH

Mulching is a gardening practice that involves covering the soil surface around plants with a layer of material. This simple yet effective technique offers numerous benefits for your herb garden. One of the primary advantages of mulching is moisture retention. By covering the soil, mulch helps reduce evaporation, ensuring that your herbs have consistent access to water. This is particularly beneficial during hot, dry spells when water can quickly evaporate from the soil surface. Additionally, mulch acts as an insulator, regulating soil temperature. It keeps the soil cooler during the scorching summer months and warmer during the chilly winter, protecting the roots from extreme temperature fluctuations.

Weed suppression is another significant benefit of mulching. A thick layer of mulch creates a barrier that prevents weed seeds from germinating and establishing themselves in your garden. This reduces the competition for nutrients, water, and sunlight, allowing your herbs to thrive without the constant battle against unwanted plants. Mulching also adds organic matter to the soil as it decomposes, enriching the soil with nutrients and improving its structure. This organic matter enhances soil fertility, promotes microbial activity, and supports healthy root development.

There are various types of mulches you can use in your herb garden, each with its own set of advantages. Organic mulches, such as straw, grass clippings, and compost, are popular choices. These materials decompose over time, adding valuable nutrients to the soil and improving its texture. Straw is particularly effective at retaining moisture and suppressing weeds, while grass clippings provide a quick nutrient boost. Compost, made from decomposed organic matter, is a rich source of nutrients and helps improve soil structure.

Inorganic mulches, such as gravel and landscape fabric, offer different benefits. Gravel is excellent for improving drainage and preventing soil erosion, making it a good choice for herbs that prefer drier conditions. Landscape fabric, on the other hand, is a durable, long-lasting option that effectively suppresses weeds. It allows water and nutrients to penetrate the soil while preventing weed growth. Living mulches, like ground cover plants, are another interesting option. These low-growing plants, such as clover or creeping thyme, cover the soil surface and provide similar benefits to traditional mulches, including moisture retention and weed suppression, while also adding beauty and biodiversity to your garden.

Applying mulch correctly is essential to reap its benefits without causing harm to your plants. Start by spreading a layer of mulch around your herbs, aiming for a depth of 2 to 4 inches. This thickness is sufficient to retain moisture, suppress weeds, and regulate soil temperature. Be careful not to pile the mulch directly against the stems of your herbs, as this can lead to stem rot and other diseases. Instead, leave a small gap around the base of each plant to ensure proper air circulation. As the mulch decomposes or compacts over time, replenish it to maintain the desired depth and continue benefiting your garden.

The long-term benefits of mulching extend beyond immediate improvements in moisture retention and weed suppression. Mulching plays a vital role in improving soil structure. As organic mulches decompose, they add organic matter to the soil, enhancing its texture and fertility. This organic matter improves the soil's ability to retain moisture and nutrients, creating a more favorable environment for root growth. Enhanced microbial activity is another significant advantage of mulching. The organic matter in mulch provides a food source for beneficial microorganisms, which play a crucial role in breaking down organic material and releasing nutrients into the soil. This microbial activity contributes to the overall health and fertility of your soil.

Mulching also helps reduce soil erosion by protecting the soil surface from the impact of raindrops and wind. This is particularly important in areas prone to heavy rainfall or strong winds, where soil erosion can be a significant problem. By maintaining a layer of mulch, you can prevent soil displacement and ensure that your valuable topsoil remains in place. Additionally, the organic matter added by mulch increases the soil's ability to hold water, reducing runoff and further preventing erosion.

Increased organic matter content is another long-term benefit of mulching. As the mulch breaks down, it adds valuable nutrients and organic material to the soil. This continuous addition of organic matter improves soil fertility, supports healthy plant growth, and enhances the overall health of your garden. By incorporating mulching into your gardening routine, you create a sustainable, nutrient-rich environment for your herbs, ensuring their long-term health and productivity.

By understanding the benefits of mulching and applying it correctly, you can significantly enhance the health and productivity of your herb garden. Whether you choose organic, inorganic, or living mulches, each type offers unique advantages that contribute to moisture retention, weed suppression, soil temperature regulation, and improved soil structure. With proper mulching techniques, you'll create a thriving, sustainable garden that supports the growth of your culinary and medicinal herbs.

3.4 MAINTAINING SOIL PH AND NUTRIENT BALANCE

The importance of soil pH in herb gardening cannot be overstated. Soil pH measures the acidity or alkalinity of your soil, which directly impacts nutrient availability to your plants. Most herbs thrive in a pH range of 6.0 to 7.0. Within this range, nutrients like nitrogen, phosphorus, and potassium are readily available, supporting robust growth. If the soil becomes too acidic, below 6.0, certain nutrients can become locked up, making them inaccessible to your herbs. This condition, known as nutrient lockout, can stunt growth and reduce the overall health of your plants. Conversely, alkaline soils, with a pH above 7.0, can lead to micronutrient deficiencies. Elements like iron, manganese, and zinc become less available, causing symptoms like chlorosis, where leaves turn yellow due to insufficient chlorophyll.

Testing your soil's pH is a straightforward process that can save you a lot of trouble down the road. DIY pH test kits are widely available and easy to use. These kits typically include a test tube, a pH test solution, and color charts to compare your results. Simply mix a soil sample with water and the test solution, and then compare the resulting color to the chart. For more precise results, professional soil testing services can provide a detailed analysis of your soil's pH and nutrient levels. These services often include recommendations for amendments based on your specific results. Additionally, investing in a pH meter can be beneficial for regular monitoring. These meters are simple to use and provide accurate readings, allowing you to make timely adjustments.

Adjusting soil pH can be necessary to create an optimal growing environment for your herbs. If your soil is too acidic, lowering the pH can be achieved by adding sulfur or organic matter. Sulfur, when applied to the soil, is converted by soil bacteria into sulfuric acid, which lowers the pH. Organic matter, such as compost or well-rotted manure, can also help to gradually lower soil pH while improving soil structure and fertility. On the other hand, if your soil is too alkaline, you can raise the pH by applying lime. Agricultural lime, made from crushed limestone, is commonly used to increase soil pH. It neutralizes acidity and provides essential calcium to the soil. Wood ash is another option, though it should be used sparingly to avoid over-alkalizing the soil. Regularly re-testing your soil's pH and adjusting as needed ensures that your herbs remain in an environment conducive to healthy growth.

Nutrients play a pivotal role in soil health and plant vitality. Macronutrients, including nitrogen, phosphorus, and potassium, are required in larger quantities for essential plant functions. Nitrogen promotes leafy growth and is vital for photosynthesis. Phosphorus supports root development and flowering, while potassium enhances overall plant health and disease resistance. In addition to these macronutrients, secondary nutrients like calcium, magnesium, and sulfur are crucial. Calcium is necessary for cell wall strength, magnesium is a core component of chlorophyll, and sulfur is important for protein synthesis. Micronutrients, though needed in smaller amounts, are equally vital. Iron, manganese, and zinc are involved in various enzymatic and metabolic processes within the plant.

Maintaining a nutrient balance in your soil is key to ensuring your herbs receive all the elements they need to thrive. Regularly adding compost to your garden is one of the simplest and most effective ways to achieve this balance. Compost enriches the soil with a broad spectrum of nutrients and improves soil structure, making it easier for plant roots to access these nutrients. Using organic fertilizers can also help maintain nutrient levels. Products like fish emulsion, bone meal, and seaweed extract provide specific nutrients that may be lacking in your soil. Crop rotation and cover cropping are additional techniques to replenish soil nutrients.

Rotating different types of crops each season helps prevent nutrient depletion and reduces the buildup of pests and diseases. Cover crops, such as legumes, can fix nitrogen in the soil, enhancing fertility for future plantings.

By understanding the importance of soil pH and nutrient balance, and by implementing these practices, you create a fertile environment where your herbs can thrive. Properly managing soil pH ensures that nutrients are available when your plants need them, while regular soil amendments and crop management practices keep your soil healthy and productive. These steps form the foundation of a successful herb garden, supporting vigorous growth and abundant harvests.

With a well-balanced soil and an effective watering strategy, you're well on your way to a thriving herb garden. Next, we'll explore the specifics of growing herbs in different climates, ensuring your garden flourishes no matter where you live.

CHAPTER 4
GROWING HERBS IN DIFFERENT CLIMATES

This chapter will guide you through the unique difficulties of growing herbs in various climates, starting with hot and dry regions.

4.1 GROWING HERBS IN HOT AND DRY CLIMATES

Gardening in hot and dry climates presents specific challenges that can test even the most seasoned gardeners. High temperatures and low humidity are the primary hurdles. The intense heat accelerates water evaporation from both the soil and the plants, making it difficult to maintain adequate moisture levels. This can lead to heat stress, where plants exhibit symptoms like wilting, yellowing leaves, and stunted growth. Limited water availability further complicates the situation, especially in areas prone to drought or water restrictions. These conditions necessitate a strategic approach to watering and plant selection to ensure your garden thrives.

Choosing the right herbs for arid conditions is the first step towards a successful garden. Drought-tolerant herbs are well-suited to withstand the harsh environment and require less frequent watering. Rosemary is an excellent choice; its woody stems and needle-like leaves are adapted to conserve water. Thyme, another Mediterranean native, thrives in dry soil and full sun. Sage, with its silvery leaves, reflects sunlight and retains moisture, making it a resilient option. Oregano, known for its robust flavor, is also well-suited to hot, dry climates. These herbs not only survive but flourish in conditions that might challenge less hardy plants.

Efficient water management is crucial in dry climates. Deep watering methods are particularly effective. This involves watering the plants thoroughly but less frequently, encouraging roots to grow deeper into the soil where moisture is more consistent. Drip irrigation systems are ideal for this purpose. They deliver water directly to the root zone, minimizing evaporation and ensuring that each plant receives the right amount of hydration. Mulching is another essential technique. A thick layer of organic mulch, such as straw or wood chips, helps retain soil moisture by reducing evaporation and keeping the soil cooler. This not only conserves water but also improves soil structure over time as the mulch decomposes.

Protecting your herbs from the intense heat is equally important. Shade cloths can be used to shield plants from the hottest part of the day, reducing the risk of heat stress. These cloths are available in different densities, allowing you to control the amount of sunlight that reaches your plants. Planting herbs in areas that receive partial shade can also help. For instance, placing your garden near taller plants or structures that cast afternoon shade can provide relief from the scorching sun. Creating windbreaks is another effective strategy. Planting shrubs or using fencing can reduce the drying effects of hot winds, helping to maintain soil moisture and protect delicate foliage.

Incorporating these practices into your gardening routine will help you create a thriving herb garden, even in the most challenging hot and dry climates. Selecting drought-tolerant herbs, employing efficient watering methods, and providing protection from extreme heat are key to ensuring your plants not only survive but thrive. With careful planning and attention to detail, you can cultivate a bountiful herb garden that provides fresh, flavorful, and medicinally beneficial herbs, no matter how harsh the conditions.

Reflection Section: Hot and Dry Climate Gardening

- **Think about your local climate**: How often do you experience high temperatures and low humidity? Reflect on how this affects your current garden.

- **Evaluate your watering methods**: Are you using deep watering techniques or drip irrigation? Consider how you can improve water efficiency in your garden.
- **Assess your plant selection**: Are you growing herbs that are well-suited to your climate? Make a list of drought-tolerant herbs you could incorporate into your garden.
- **Plan for shade and wind protection**: Look at your garden layout. Are there opportunities to provide shade or create windbreaks to protect your herbs from extreme heat?

4.2 ADAPTING HERB GARDENING TO COLD AND FROSTY REGIONS

Gardening in cold and frosty regions brings its own set of challenges. Frost damage is a significant concern, as freezing temperatures can injure or kill tender plants. When frost hits, water inside plant cells expands, causing the cells to burst. This results in blackened, wilted leaves and stems. Another issue is the short growing season. In colder climates, the window for planting, growing, and harvesting is limited, which can be frustrating when you're eager to see your garden flourish. Additionally, soil freezing during winter can make it difficult for roots to access water and nutrients, leading to stunted growth or even plant death.

Despite these challenges, certain herbs are well-suited to withstand low temperatures and frost. Chives are a hardy perennial that can survive harsh winters. They go dormant in the cold but come back to life in the spring, making them a reliable addition to your garden. Mint is another resilient herb. While it may die back in severe frost, its roots remain viable underground, ready to sprout again when the weather warms. Parsley is surprisingly cold-tolerant and can continue growing even after a light frost. Thyme, with its woody stems and small, tough leaves, is well-adapted to survive frosty conditions. These herbs can provide fresh flavors and medicinal benefits year-round, even in colder climates.

Protecting your herbs from frost damage requires some strategic interventions. Row covers and cloches are excellent tools for shielding plants from the cold. Row covers are lightweight, fabric-like materials that you can drape over your plants to trap heat and protect them from frost. Cloches are bell-shaped covers, tradition-ally made of glass, that serve the same purpose. Both can be placed over your herbs during cold nights and removed during the day to allow sunlight and air circulation. Heavy mulching is another effective method. Applying a thick layer of mulch around the base of your plants insulates the soil, keeping it warmer and reducing the risk of root damage. Mulch also helps retain soil moisture, which can be beneficial during dry winter periods.

For potted herbs, bringing them indoors before the first frost can save them from the harsh winter conditions. Place them in a sunny spot, such as a south-facing window, where they can continue to receive adequate light. If indoor space is limited, consider using compact grow lights to supplement natural light. Regularly check the soil moisture and avoid overwatering, as indoor environments can cause soil to dry out more slowly. This simple step can extend the life of your herbs and keep them productive through the winter months.

Extending the growing season in cold climates involves a few proactive strategies. Starting seeds indoors is a practical approach. By sowing seeds indoors several weeks before the last expected frost, you give your herbs a head start. Use seed trays or small pots filled with a seed-starting mix, and place them in a warm, well-lit area. Once the seedlings are strong enough, gradually acclimate them to outdoor conditions before transplanting them into your garden. Cold frames and greenhouses are valuable tools for extending the growing season. Cold frames are simple, unheated structures with a transparent lid that traps solar energy, creating a microclimate that's warmer than the surrounding area. Green-houses offer even more protection, allowing you to grow herbs year-round. Both can be used to start seeds earlier in the season and to keep plants growing later into the fall.

Planting in raised beds can also help warm the soil faster in the spring. Raised beds elevate the soil above ground level, allowing it to drain and warm up more quickly than in-ground beds. This can give you a head start on the growing season and provide better conditions for your herbs. Consider using dark-colored materials for your raised beds, as they absorb more heat from the sun, further warming the soil. These methods can help you make the most of the growing season, even in cold and frosty regions.

By understanding and addressing the challenges of cold climates, you can create a thriving herb garden that provides fresh, flavor-ful, and medicinally beneficial herbs throughout the year.

4.3 HERB GARDENING IN HUMID AND TROPICAL CLIMATES

High humidity and tropical climates can create unique challenges for herb gardeners. One of the most significant issues is the exces-sive moisture that these environments generate. High humidity can lead to mold and mildew, which thrive in damp conditions. These fungal diseases can quickly spread and damage your plants, causing leaves to yellow and weaken. Additionally, the warm, moist environment encourages increased pest activity. Insects such as aphids, spider mites, and whiteflies can become more prevalent, feeding on your herbs and spreading diseases. Soil compaction from heavy rains is another concern. When the soil becomes too dense, it restricts root growth and reduces the soil's ability to absorb and drain water effectively.

Despite these challenges, certain herbs thrive in high humidity. Lemongrass is a fantastic option for humid environments. It loves the moisture and can grow quite tall, adding a beautiful, tropical look to your garden. Ginger is another excellent choice. This aromatic root prefers warm, humid conditions and can be harvested for both culinary and medicinal uses. Basil, a staple in many kitchens, also does well in humid climates, provided it gets enough air circulation to prevent fungal issues. Turmeric, with its vibrant orange root, thrives in the warm, wet conditions typical of tropical regions. Each of these herbs brings unique flavors and health benefits to your garden, making them worthy additions.

Managing pests and diseases in humid climates requires a proactive approach. Ensuring proper air circulation around your plants is crucial. Space your herbs adequately to allow airflow and reduce the risk of fungal diseases. Pruning can also help by removing excess foliage that might trap moisture. Using organic fungicides like neem oil or copper-based sprays can effectively manage fungal infections without harming beneficial insects. Regular inspection of your plants is vital. Check the undersides of leaves, where pests often hide, and look for any signs of disease. Early detection allows for prompt action, preventing minor issues from becoming major problems. Implementing these strategies can help keep your herbs healthy and productive in a humid environment.

Soil management in tropical climates is equally important. Heavy rains can lead to waterlogging and nutrient leaching, making it essential to improve soil drainage. Adding organic matter such as compost or well-rotted manure can enhance soil structure and increase its ability to drain excess water. This organic matter also provides essential nutrients, supporting robust plant growth. Raised beds are another effective solution. By elevating your garden beds, you allow excess water to drain more easily, preventing the roots from sitting in waterlogged soil. Regularly testing your soil's pH and nutrient levels helps you make informed decisions about amendments. Tropical soils can sometimes become more acidic due to heavy rainfall, so periodic lime applications may be necessary to maintain optimal pH levels.

Incorporating these techniques into your gardening routine will help you cultivate a thriving herb garden in humid and tropical climates. By selecting suitable herbs, managing pests and diseases proactively, and improving soil conditions, you can overcome the challenges posed by excessive moisture and heavy rains. This approach will ensure your garden remains healthy and productive, providing you with fresh, flavorful, and medicinally beneficial herbs year-round.

Visual Element: Pest and Disease Management Checklist

- **Ensure Proper Air Circulation**: Space plants adequately and prune to remove excess foliage.
- **Use Organic Fungicides**: Apply neem oil or copper-based sprays as needed.
- **Regular Inspections**: Check plants for pests and disease signs weekly.
- **Improve Soil Drainage**: Add organic matter and use raised beds.
- **Test Soil Regularly**: Monitor pH and nutrient levels to maintain optimal conditions.

These steps will help you manage the increased risks of pests and diseases in humid environments, ensuring your herb garden remains vibrant and healthy.

4.4 STRATEGIES FOR GROWING HERBS IN COASTAL AREAS

Gardening in coastal areas presents its own unique hurdle. The proximity to the ocean means that your garden is constantly exposed to salt spray, which can cause salt damage to plants. Salt can accumulate in the soil and on the leaves of your herbs, leading to dehydration and nutrient imbalances. Wind exposure is another significant issue. Coastal winds can be strong and relentless, causing physical damage to plants and increasing the rate of water evaporation from the soil. Additionally, sandy soils common in coastal regions are often nutrient poor. They drain quickly, which means nutrients are leached away before plants have a chance to absorb them. This combination of salt, wind, and poor soil can make coastal gardening seem daunting, but with the right strategies, you can create a thriving herb garden.

Choosing the right herbs is the first step to overcoming these challenges. Some herbs are naturally more tolerant of salt and can thrive in coastal conditions. Rosemary is a fantastic choice. It's tough, needle-like leaves are well-adapted to withstand salt spray and wind. Lavender is another excellent option. With its fragrant flowers and silvery foliage, it not only adds beauty to your garden but also handles salt exposure with ease. Thyme, with its small, resilient leaves, is well-suited to coastal environments. It forms a low-growing mat that can help protect the soil from erosion. Oregano, known for its robust growth and flavorful leaves, is also quite salt-tolerant. These herbs not only survive but flourish in coastal conditions, providing both culinary and medicinal benefits.

Protecting your herbs from wind and salt spray involves creating physical barriers. Planting windbreaks or hedges around your garden can significantly reduce wind exposure. Shrubs and small trees can act as a buffer, slowing down the wind and providing a more sheltered environment for your herbs. Using protective barriers like burlap screens can also help. These screens can be placed around individual plants or along the perimeter of your garden to shield them from the worst of the wind and salt spray. Growing herbs in pots is another effective strategy. Containers allow you to move your plants as needed to protect them from harsh conditions. During particularly windy or stormy weather, you can relocate your pots to a more sheltered area, such as a porch or greenhouse.

Improving sandy soils is crucial for providing your herbs with the nutrients they need to thrive. Adding compost and organic matter to sandy soil can significantly enhance its nutrient retention and structure. Compost not only provides essential nutrients but also improves the soil's ability to hold water, reducing the frequency of watering needed. Mixing well-rotted manure or leaf mold into the soil can further enhance its fertility. Mulching is another effective technique. A layer of organic mulch, such as straw or wood chips, helps reduce soil erosion by protecting the surface from wind and rain. It also conserves moisture and gradually breaks down, adding more organic matter to the soil.

Using slow-release organic fertilizers can provide your herbs with a steady supply of nutrients. Products like fish emulsion, bone meal, and seaweed extract are excellent choices. These fertilizers release nutrients slowly over time, ensuring that your plants have access to what they need without the risk of nutrient leaching. Regularly testing your soil's nutrient levels can help you make informed decisions about when and how much fertilizer to apply. This proactive approach ensures that your herbs receive consistent nourishment, supporting healthy growth and productivity.

By understanding and addressing the specific challenges of coastal gardening, you can create a thriving herb garden that withstands the harsh conditions. Selecting salt-tolerant herbs, protecting them from wind and salt spray, and improving sandy soils are key strategies for success. With these practices in place, your coastal herb garden will not only survive but thrive, providing you with an abundance of fresh, flavorful, and health beneficial herbs.

In our next chapter, we will explore the best practices for seasonal planting and harvesting, ensuring you get the most out of your garden year-round.

Reflection Section: Coastal Gardening Strategies

- **Evaluate your garden's exposure to wind and salt spray**: Consider planting windbreaks or using burlap screens to protect your herbs.
- **Assess your soil quality**: Is it sandy and nutrient-poor? Plan to add compost and organic matter to improve its structure and fertility.
- **Consider container gardening**: Growing herbs in pots can provide flexibility to move them as needed to protect from harsh coastal conditions.
- **Choose salt-tolerant herbs**: Make a list of herbs like rosemary, lavender, thyme, and oregano that are well-suited to coastal environments.

CHAPTER 5
SEASONAL PLANTING
AND HARVESTING

This chapter will guide you through the essentials of seasonal planting and harvesting, starting with the critical steps to get a head start in the spring.

5.1 SPRING PLANTING: GETTING A HEAD START

Spring is a season of renewal, and your herb garden is no exception. Early planning and preparation are the keys to making the most of this vibrant time of year. As winter draws to a close, start by creating a planting calendar. This tool helps you organize your gardening tasks and ensures you don't miss crucial planting windows. Note the last expected frost date in your area and plan to start seeds indoors about six to eight weeks before this date. A planting calendar keeps you on track and allows you to stagger plantings for a continuous harvest.

Preparing your garden beds and containers in late winter sets the stage for a successful growing season. Clear away any debris from the previous year and test your soil to determine its pH and nutrient levels. Amend the soil as needed with compost or organic fertilizers to create a fertile environment for your herbs. If you're using containers, clean them thoroughly and fill them with fresh potting mix. This preparation ensures that your herbs have the best possible start when the weather warms up. Ordering seeds and supplies early is another critical step. Popular varieties can sell out quickly, and having your seeds on hand allows you to start them indoors without delay.

Spring is an ideal time to plant certain herbs that thrive in the cooler temperatures of early spring. Cilantro is one such herb. It prefers the mild weather of spring and can bolt quickly in the heat of summer. Plant it early to enjoy its fresh, citrusy leaves before the temperatures rise. Dill is another excellent choice for spring planting. It grows best in cool weather and can be sown directly into the garden once the soil is workable. Parsley, a versatile herb, germinates well in the cool, moist conditions of spring. Chervil, with its delicate anise flavor, also thrives in the mild temperatures of early spring. These herbs not only enhance your culinary creations but also support your health with their unique medicinal properties.

To ensure a successful spring garden, start your seeds indoors using seed trays and grow lights. Fill the trays with a seed-starting mix, which is lighter and more sterile than regular potting soil. Plant the seeds according to the depth recommendations on the packet and water them gently. Place the trays under grow lights, keeping the lights just a few inches above the seedlings. Maintain an optimal temperature of around 70°F and ensure good air circulation to prevent fungal issues. Consistent humidity is also essential for germination, so cover the trays with a plastic dome or wrap them in plastic until the seeds sprout.

Once your seedlings have grown strong enough, it's time to harden them off before transplanting them into the garden. This process gradually acclimates the young plants to outdoor conditions, reducing the risk of transplant shock. Start by placing the seedlings outside in a sheltered, shady spot for a few hours each day. Gradually increase their exposure to sunlight and outdoor temperatures over the course of a week or two. This slow transition helps the plants adjust to the harsher outdoor environment and prepares them for a successful transplant.

Early-season care, and maintenance are crucial for nurturing your young plants during the spring. Water your newly planted herbs regularly, ensuring the soil remains consistently moist but not waterlogged. Spring weather can be unpredictable, with sudden frosts posing a risk to tender seedlings. Protect them by covering them with row covers or cloches during cold nights. These protective measures trap heat and shield the plants from freezing temperatures. Mulching early in the season helps retain soil moisture and suppresses weeds. Apply a layer of organic mulch, such as straw or wood chips, around your plants to keep the soil cool and reduce the need for frequent watering.

Spring is a time of rapid growth and renewal. By planning ahead, preparing your garden beds, and selecting the right herbs, you set the stage for a productive and enjoyable growing season. Whether you're starting seeds indoors or planting directly in the garden, these early-season strategies ensure your herbs get off to a strong start. With consistent care and attention, you'll soon be rewarded with a bountiful harvest of fresh, flavorful, and medicinally beneficial herbs.

5.2 SUMMER CARE AND MAINTENANCE

Summer brings with it high temperatures and potential drought conditions. Managing these factors is crucial to ensuring your herbs thrive. One of the most effective strategies is to implement efficient watering systems. Drip irrigation and soaker hoses are excellent choices. They deliver water directly to the root zone, minimizing evaporation and ensuring that each plant gets the hydration it needs without wasting water. These systems are particularly useful in hot climates where water conservation is essential.

Using shade cloths to protect delicate herbs from the intense summer sun can make a significant difference. Shade cloths come in various densities, allowing you to control the amount of sunlight that reaches your plants. By reducing the amount of direct sunlight, you can prevent heat stress and sunburn on sensitive leaves. This is especially important for herbs like basil, which can wilt quickly under harsh sun. Position the shade cloths so they provide protection during the hottest part of the day, while still allowing enough light for photosynthesis.

Certain herbs are well-suited to summer's heat and can thrive even in the hottest conditions. Basil is a summer staple, flourishing in warm weather and producing abundant, fragrant leaves. Rosemary is another herb that loves the sun and can tolerate dry conditions, making it perfect for summer gardens. Thyme, with its small, resilient leaves, also thrives in hot weather and is less demanding when it comes to water. Sage, with its gray-green leaves, is not only drought-tolerant but also adds a lovely visual element to your garden. These herbs are robust and can handle the challenges that summer presents.

Regular maintenance is essential during the summer months. Pruning and pinching back herbs encourage bushy growth and prevent them from becoming leggy. For example, pinching back the tops of basil plants encourages them to branch out, resulting in a fuller plant. This practice also delays flowering, which can cause the flavor of the leaves to change. Monitoring for pests and diseases is another crucial task. The warm weather can attract a variety of insects, such as aphids and spider mites. Regularly inspect your plants and address any issues promptly. Using organic pest control methods, such as neem oil or insecticidal soap, can help keep your herbs healthy without resorting to harsh chemicals.

Fertilizing your herbs with organic compost tea during the summer provides them with a nutrient boost. Compost tea is made by steeping compost in water, creating a nutrient-rich liquid that you can apply to your plants. This method not only feeds your herbs but also improves soil health. Apply compost tea every few weeks to support vigorous growth and enhance the flavor of your herbs. It's a simple yet effective way to ensure your plants are getting the nutrients they need during the peak growing season.

Harvesting herbs throughout the summer is a rewarding task that ensures continuous growth and abundant yields. Basil should be harvested frequently to prevent it from bolting or going to seed. Regularly picking the leaves encourages the plant to produce more foliage. When harvesting basil, remove the top few inches of the plant, just above a leaf node. This practice promotes new growth and keeps the plant healthy. Mint, another prolific grower, should be cut just above a leaf node to encourage branching. This method helps maintain a bushy, productive plant. Rosemary can be harvested as needed for culinary use. Simply snip off a few sprigs, taking care not to remove more than a third of the plant at a time. This ensures that the plant remains healthy and continues to grow.

Summer is a time of rapid growth and abundant harvests. By implementing efficient watering systems, using shade cloths, and choosing herbs that thrive in hot weather, you can overcome the challenges of summer gardening. Regular maintenance, including pruning, pest monitoring, and fertilizing, keeps your herbs healthy and productive. Harvesting frequently not only provides you with a steady supply of fresh herbs but also encourages continuous growth. With these strategies, your summer garden will flourish, offering a bounty of flavorful and medicinally beneficial herbs.

5.3 FALL HARVESTING AND PREPARING FOR WINTER

As the days grow shorter and the air takes on a crispness, it's time to think about the final harvest. This is your last chance to make the most of the season's growth before winter sets in. Timing the final harvest is crucial for capturing the peak flavor and potency of your herbs. Herbs like oregano and thyme should be harvested just before the first frost. This timing ensures they are at their most flavorful. To harvest these herbs, clip the stems in the morning after the dew has dried but before the heat of the day. This preserves the essential oils responsible for their rich aromas and flavors.

After harvesting, drying your herbs is an excellent way to preserve them for winter use. For herbs like oregano and thyme, you can use a dehydrator. This method is quick and efficient, retaining much of the herbs' flavor and potency. If you prefer a more traditional approach, air drying is also effective. Bundle the stems together and hang them upside down in a warm, dry place with good air circulation. Once dried, store the herbs in airtight containers away from light and heat to maintain their quality. Another method is freezing herbs in ice cube trays filled with olive oil. This is particularly useful for herbs like basil, which can lose flavor when dried. Simply chop the herbs, place them in the trays, cover with olive oil, and freeze. When you need a burst of fresh herb flavor, pop a cube into your cooking.

Making herb-infused oils and vinegars is another way to preserve your harvest. To make herb-infused oil, start by choosing a light, neutral oil like olive or grapeseed oil. Add fresh herbs, ensuring they are completely submerged to prevent mold growth. Seal the container and store it in a cool, dark place for a few weeks, shaking it occasionally. Strain the oil and transfer it to a clean bottle for long-term storage. Herb-infused vinegars follow a similar process. Use white wine vinegar or apple cider vinegar as a base. Add your herbs, seal the container, and let it infuse for a few weeks. Strain and bottle the vinegar, which can add a delightful flavor to salads and marinades.

Preparing your garden for winter is essential for protecting your plants and ensuring a good start next spring. Mulching heavily around the base of your perennial herbs insulates the roots from freezing temperatures. Use organic materials like straw, leaves, or wood chips. This layer of mulch not only protects the roots but also helps retain moisture in the soil. Covering your perennial herbs with frost blankets provides additional protection. These blankets trap heat and shield the plants from cold winds and frost. Secure the blankets with stakes or rocks to keep them in place throughout the winter.

Cleaning up your garden beds is another important step. Remove any dead plant material, as it can harbor pests and diseases over the winter. Compost the plant debris or dispose of it if you suspect it's diseased. This cleanup helps create a healthier environment for your plants in the coming season. After cleaning up, consider adding a layer of compost to your garden beds. This enriches the soil and prepares it for spring planting.

Fall is also an excellent time for planting certain herbs that will give you a head start next spring. Garlic is a prime example. Plant garlic cloves in the fall, a few weeks before the ground freezes. They will establish roots over the winter and be ready for harvest in early summer. Chives can also be planted in the fall. They are hardy and will start growing as soon as the weather warms up. Parsley, though often treated as an annual, can be planted in the fall for an early spring harvest. Cilantro, which bolts quickly in the heat, thrives in the cool temperatures of fall and early spring.

By making the most of the final harvest, preserving your herbs, and preparing your garden for winter, you ensure a continuous supply of fresh, flavorful, and medicinally beneficial herbs. These practices not only extend the use of your herbs throughout the year but also set the stage for a vibrant and productive garden when spring returns.

5.4 WINTER HERB GARDENING: INDOOR AND GREENHOUSE TECHNIQUES

Winter doesn't have to signal the end of your herb gardening endeavors. Growing herbs indoors during the colder months comes with several benefits, making it an attractive option for many gardeners. One of the most obvious advantages is the availability of fresh herbs year-round. Imagine plucking fresh basil leaves in the dead of winter to add a burst of flavor to your dishes. Indoor gardening also protects your plants from harsh winter weather. Snow, frost, and freezing temperatures won't touch your indoor garden. Additionally, you have better control over the growing conditions. You can regulate the light, temperature, and humidity to create an ideal environment for your herbs.

Setting up an indoor herb garden requires some initial planning but is quite manageable. Start by choosing suitable containers. These should have good drainage to prevent waterlogged soil, which can lead to root rot. Terracotta pots are a good option as they are porous and allow for better airflow. Fill these containers with high-quality potting soil that's rich in organic matter. Avoid using garden soil, as it's often too heavy and can harbor pests.

Adequate light is crucial for indoor herbs. Place your containers in a sunny window, preferably one that faces south or west and receives at least six hours of sunlight daily. If natural light is insufficient, invest in grow lights. LED grow lights are energy-efficient and provide the full spectrum of light that plants need. Position the lights about 6-12 inches above the plants and keep them on for 12-16 hours a day to mimic natural sunlight.

Maintaining the right humidity and ventilation is also essential. Indoor air can be dry, especially in winter when heating systems are in use. To maintain adequate humidity, you can use a humidifier or place a tray of water near your plants. Grouping plants together can also help increase humidity levels. Ensure good air circulation by occasionally opening windows or using a small fan. This helps prevent fungal diseases and keeps your plants healthy.

Greenhouse gardening offers another excellent way to extend your growing season through winter. A greenhouse provides a controlled environment where you can grow herbs year-round. Heating options for greenhouses vary, from electric heaters to passive solar heating. Electric heaters are effective but can be costly to run. Passive solar heating uses the sun's energy to warm the greenhouse, reducing energy costs. Insulate your greenhouse with bubble wrap or thermal screens to retain heat.

Ventilation is just as important in a greenhouse as it is indoors. Proper airflow helps control humidity and prevents mold and mildew. Use vents or fans to ensure air circulates effectively. In colder climates, cold frames within the greenhouse offer extra protection. These are essentially mini greenhouses that trap additional heat, safeguarding your herbs from freezing temperatures. Cold frames are particularly useful for starting seeds early or extending the harvest of cold-tolerant herbs.

Certain herbs thrive in controlled environments, making them ideal for indoor or greenhouse gardening. Basil is a top choice; it loves the warm, stable conditions provided by an indoor garden or greenhouse. Mint is another excellent option. It's vigorous and can adapt well to indoor conditions, provided it gets enough light and water. Parsley, with its hardy nature, grows well indoors and can be harvested continuously. Chives are also well-suited for indoor gardening. They require minimal space and can thrive in pots on a sunny windowsill.

By taking advantage of indoor and greenhouse gardening techniques, you can enjoy fresh herbs all winter long. These methods provide a sanctuary for your plants, protecting them from the harsh elements and giving you control over their growing conditions. Whether you choose to grow your herbs on a sunny windowsill or in a well-equipped greenhouse, you'll find that winter herb gardening is both rewarding and practical.

Planting and harvesting herbs according to the seasons not only ensures a continuous supply of fresh, flavorful, and health beneficial herbs, but also enhances your gardening experience. The next chapter will delve into organic pest and disease control, providing strategies to keep your herb garden healthy and productive year-round.

CHAPTER 6
ORGANIC PEST AND DISEASE CONTROL

In this chapter, we will explore how to identify common herb pests and implement effective, organic strategies to protect your garden.

6.1 IDENTIFYING COMMON HERB PESTS

Herb gardens, while generally resilient, are not immune to pests. Understanding the common culprits and their behaviors is the first step in managing them effectively. Aphids, spider mites, whiteflies, and slugs and snails are among the most frequent invaders. Aphids are small, soft-bodied insects that come in various colors, including green, black, and pink. They are often found clustered on new growth, where they suck sap from the plant tissues. This feeding weakens the plants and causes the foliage to curl and distort. The sticky honeydew they excrete can also promote the growth of sooty mold, further compromising plant health.

Spider Mites

Spider mites are another common pest, particularly in hot and dry conditions. These tiny arachnids are barely visible to the naked eye but can cause significant damage. They feed by piercing plant cells and sucking out their contents, leading to the appearance of yellow or white speckles on the leaves. A telltale sign of a spider mite infestation is the presence of fine webbing on the undersides of the leaves. Left unchecked, spider mites can cause extensive damage, leading to leaf drop and reduced plant vigor.

Whiteflies

Whiteflies are small, winged insects that thrive in warm climates. They congregate on the undersides of leaves, where they lay their eggs. When disturbed, they take flight in a cloud of tiny white insects. Like aphids, whiteflies feed on plant sap, causing leaves to yellow and weaken. Their honeydew secretion can also attract ants and support the growth of sooty mold.

Snails

Slugs and snails are more of a problem in moist environments. These mollusks are nocturnal feeders, emerging at night to munch on tender leaves and stems. They leave behind irregular holes in the foliage and a telltale slime trail. Slugs and snails can cause significant damage, especially to young seedlings and low-growing herbs.

Early detection of these pests is crucial for effective control. Regular visual inspections are your first line of defense. Take the time to examine the undersides of leaves and plant stems, where many pests like to hide. Look for signs of feeding damage, such as curled leaves, speckled foliage, and sticky honeydew. Yellow sticky traps can be useful for monitoring flying pests like whiteflies. These traps attract and capture the insects, allowing you to gauge the severity of the infestation.

For slugs and snails, beer traps are a simple and effective method. Bury shallow containers filled with beer at soil level near your plants. The scent of the beer attracts slugs and snails, which then fall in and drown. Regularly check and replenish these traps to keep their numbers in check.

Understanding the life cycles and behaviors of these pests can inform your control strategies. Aphids reproduce rapidly, with multiple generations in a single growing season. They are particularly attracted to new growth, so monitoring these areas closely is essential. Spider mites thrive in hot, dry conditions, making them more of a problem during the summer months. Increasing humidity around your plants can help deter them. Whiteflies lay their eggs on the undersides of leaves, so keeping an eye on these areas can help you catch an infestation early. Slugs and snails are most active during cool, moist conditions, typically at night. Removing garden debris and creating barriers can help reduce their habitat and limit their access to your plants.

By being vigilant and proactive, you can manage these common herb pests effectively. Regular inspections, early detection, and a good understanding of pest behaviors are key to maintaining a healthy and productive herb garden.

6.2 NATURAL REMEDIES FOR PEST CONTROL

Integrated Pest Management (IPM) is a cornerstone of organic gardening, combining multiple strategies to manage pest populations effectively while minimizing harm to the environment. It emphasizes long-term prevention and control by integrating biological, cultural, physical, and chemical methods. This approach reduces the reliance on chemical pesticides, promoting a healthier garden ecosystem. Biological controls involve using natural predators and beneficial organisms to keep pest populations in check.

Cultural controls focus on creating an environment that discourages pests, such as crop rotation and proper plant spacing. Physical controls include barriers and traps to exclude or remove pests, while chemical controls, used as a last resort, involve organic and less toxic substances.

Physical control methods are straightforward but effective. Hand-picking pests off plants is a simple yet impactful way to manage small infestations. This method is particularly useful for larger pests like slugs and snails, which can be easily spotted and removed. Row covers are another excellent physical barrier. Made from lightweight fabric, they protect your herbs from flying insects while allowing light and moisture to penetrate. These covers are ideal for plants prone to aphid and whitefly attacks. Copper tape is a handy tool for deterring slugs and snails. When placed around the rims of pots or garden beds, it creates a mild electrical charge that repels these pests, keeping them away from your precious herbs.

Biological control methods leverage nature's own pest control agents. Ladybugs are voracious predators of aphids, consuming hundreds of these pests during their lifetime. Introducing ladybugs to your garden can significantly reduce aphid populations. Predatory mites are effective against spider mites. These beneficial mites feed on spider mites, helping to control their numbers without the need for chemical sprays. Parasitic wasps are another valuable ally, particularly against whiteflies. These tiny wasps lay their eggs inside whitefly larvae, eventually killing them. Encouraging these natural predators in your garden fosters a balanced ecosystem where pests are kept in check naturally.

Homemade organic pest sprays offer a safe and effective way to manage pests using household ingredients. A garlic and chili spray works wonders against aphids and whiteflies. To make this spray, blend a few cloves of garlic and a couple of hot chili peppers with water. Strain the mixture and dilute it in a spray bottle with water. Apply it to the affected plants, ensuring you cover both the tops and undersides of the leaves. The strong scent of garlic and chili deters the pests and disrupts their feeding. Neem oil is a versatile organic pesticide that works against a wide range of pests, including aphids, spider mites, and whiteflies. Derived from the seeds of the neem tree, it disrupts the life cycle of insects, preventing them from feeding, molting, or reproducing. Mix neem oil with water and a few drops of dish soap to help it adhere to the leaves, then spray it on your plants as needed.

A simple soap and water spray is effective against soft-bodied insects like aphids. Mix a few drops of mild liquid soap in a spray bottle filled with water. Spray the solution directly onto the pests, ensuring thorough coverage. The soap suffocates the insects by breaking down their protective outer layer. This method is gentle on your plants and can be used regularly to keep pest populations under control.

By integrating these natural remedies and IPM principles, you can create a resilient and healthy herb garden. Combining biological, cultural, physical, and chemical controls ensures a balanced approach to pest management. Hand-picking pests, using row covers, and installing copper tape provide immediate physical barriers. Encouraging beneficial insects like ladybugs, predatory mites, and parasitic wasps helps maintain a natural pest control system. Homemade sprays offer a safe and effective alternative to chemical pesticides, keeping your garden thriving without harming the environment. Each of these methods contributes to a holistic strategy that supports the long-term health of your herb garden.

6.3 MANAGING HERB DISEASES ORGANICALLY

Recognizing and managing diseases early can save your plants from significant damage. Powdery mildew is one of the most common diseases affecting herbs. It manifests as white, powdery spots on the leaves, which can spread rapidly if untreated. This disease thrives in warm, dry conditions and can weaken the plant, reducing its vitality. Downy mildew, on the other hand, appears as yellow or white patches on the undersides of leaves. It prefers cooler, damp conditions and can cause the leaves to wilt and drop prematurely.

Root rot is another dreaded disease, often resulting from overwatering or poor drainage. Symptoms include wilting and yellowing leaves, accompanied by mushy, decaying roots. This disease can be particularly devastating as it affects the plant's ability to absorb water and nutrients, leading to its eventual collapse. Rust, characterized by orange or brown pustules on leaves and stems, is also a frequent visitor to herb gardens. This fungal disease can spread quickly, causing leaves to yellow and drop, significantly impacting the plant's health and productivity.

Preventing these diseases begins with adopting proactive cultural practices. Proper spacing and air circulation are crucial in minimizing the risk of fungal infections. When plants are too close together, they create a humid environment that fosters disease development. Ensure that your herbs have enough space to breathe, which helps reduce humidity and promotes healthier growth. Watering at the base of the plants, rather than overhead, keeps the leaves dry and reduces the risk of fungal diseases. This practice is especially important for herbs prone to mildew and rust.

Crop rotation is another effective strategy to prevent soil-borne diseases. By rotating the types of plants grown in a particular area each season, you disrupt the life cycle of pathogens that may be present in the soil. For example, if you grew basil in one spot last year, consider planting a different herb or vegetable in that area this year. This practice not only helps in disease prevention but also improves soil fertility and structure.

When it comes to treating herb diseases organically, several natural remedies can help manage and mitigate the impact. For powdery mildew, a simple baking soda spray can be effective. Mix one tablespoon of baking soda with a gallon of water and a few drops of liquid soap. Spray this solution on the affected leaves, ensuring thorough coverage. This remedy helps alter the pH on the leaf surface, making it inhospitable for the mildew to thrive.

Root rot can be addressed with a hydrogen peroxide soil drench. Dilute one part hydrogen peroxide with three parts water and pour it around the base of the affected plant. This solution helps oxygenate the soil, killing the anaerobic bacteria responsible for root rot. It also promotes healthier root growth and improves overall soil health. Compost tea is another valuable tool in your organic disease management arsenal. This nutrient-rich solution boosts plant immunity and helps combat various fungal diseases. To make compost tea, steep a bag of compost in a bucket of water for 24-48 hours. Strain the liquid and use it as a foliar spray to strengthen your plants' natural defenses.

Maintaining good sanitation and hygiene in your garden is crucial for disease prevention. Always remove and dispose of infected plant material promptly to prevent the spread of pathogens. This practice helps keep the disease from spreading to healthy plants. Sterilizing your tools and equipment regularly is another important step. Use a solution of one part bleach to nine parts water to disinfect your pruning shears, trowels, and other gardening tools. This simple act can significantly reduce the risk of disease transmission.

Avoid working in your garden when plants are wet, as this can spread diseases through water droplets. Fungal spores are easily transferred from plant to plant in wet conditions, so it's best to wait until the foliage is dry before handling your herbs. Regularly inspect your plants for signs of disease and act quickly to address any issues. Early intervention is key to managing herb diseases and maintaining a healthy garden.

6.4 BENEFICIAL INSECTS AND COMPANION PLANTS FOR PEST CONTROL

In my early years of gardening, I discovered a hidden army working tirelessly to keep my plants healthy. These unsung heroes were the beneficial insects that naturally controlled pests, reducing the need for chemical interventions. Ladybugs, lacewings, and predatory beetles were among the first I noticed. Ladybugs are perhaps the most well-known beneficial insect, with both adults and larvae consuming vast numbers of aphids. Lacewings, with their delicate, green wings, are voracious eaters of aphids, thrips, and caterpillars in their larval stage. Predatory beetles, such as ground beetles, patrol the soil surface at night, feasting on slugs, caterpillars, and other soft-bodied pests.

Parasitoids, like parasitic wasps and tachinid flies, play a different but equally vital role in pest control. These insects lay their eggs in or on the bodies of pest insects. When the eggs hatch, the larvae consume the host from the inside out, effectively controlling pest populations. Parasitic wasps are particularly effective against caterpillars and aphids, while tachinid flies target a wide range of insects, including beetles and moths. These beneficial insects help maintain a natural balance in the garden, reducing the need for human intervention.

Creating a welcoming habitat for these beneficial insects involves a few key practices. Plant nectar-rich flowers like yarrow, dill, and fennel. These plants provide food for adult beneficial insects, encouraging them to stay in your garden. Providing water sources is also crucial. A shallow dish filled with water and a few stones for perching can make a big difference. Additionally, creating shelter by planting a variety of flowering plants and allowing some areas of your garden to remain undisturbed gives these insects a place to live and reproduce. Reducing or eliminating pesticide use is essential, as even organic pesticides can harm beneficial insects. By fostering a supportive environment, you can attract and sustain a healthy population of natural pest controllers.

Companion planting is another powerful strategy in your pest control toolkit. Certain plant combinations can deter pests, enhance growth, and improve flavor. Basil and tomatoes are a classic pairing. The strong scent of basil repels tomato hornworms, while also enhancing the flavor of the tomatoes. Marigolds are excellent companions for many herbs, deterring nematodes and aphids with their strong scent. Planting marigolds around the perimeter of your garden can create a protective barrier against pests. Garlic, with its potent aroma, is effective at repelling aphids and Japanese beetles. Planting garlic near roses can help keep these pests at bay, ensuring your roses remain healthy and vibrant.

Several companion plant pairings stand out for their effectiveness in pest control. Nasturtiums, when planted with squash and cucumbers, repel squash bugs and cucumber beetles. The bright flowers also attract beneficial insects like predatory beetles and hoverflies. Borage, with its star-shaped blue flowers, is a great companion for strawberries. It attracts pollinators and deters pests like tomato hornworms. Chives, with their mild onion flavor, are excellent companions for carrots and roses. They help repel carrot flies and aphids, ensuring your plants grow strong and healthy. By integrating these companion plants into your garden, you create a diverse and resilient ecosystem that naturally deters pests and supports plant health.

Incorporating beneficial insects and companion plants into your pest control strategy enhances the overall health and resilience of your garden. By attracting natural predators and creating supportive habitats, you reduce the need for chemical interventions and promote a balanced ecosystem. Planting nectar-rich flowers, providing water and shelter, and minimizing pesticide use are simple yet effective ways to support beneficial insects. Pairing herbs and vegetables with compatible companions adds another layer of protection, ensuring your garden remains productive and vibrant. As you implement these practices, you'll find that your garden thrives with less effort and intervention, allowing you to enjoy the fruits of your labor with peace of mind.

By understanding and utilizing these natural pest control methods, you not only protect your herbs but also contribute to a healthier garden environment. In the next chapter, we'll explore the best practices for harvesting and preserving your herbs, ensuring they retain their flavor and potency for culinary and holistic health use.

YOUR FEEDBACK IS VALUED!

Thank you for reading *The Grinning Gardener's Handbook Volume 3: A comprehensive guide to growing organic herbs for culinary and holistic health purposes in different climates and seasons.* I hope this book has inspired you and provided valuable insights to help you cultivate a thriving organic herb garden, no matter where you live. If you found this book helpful, I'd be so grateful if you could take a moment to leave a **5-star** review on Amazon.

It costs nothing, but your review can make a world of difference in helping others, just like you, find this book. Every review not only supports my work but also increases the chances that this message will reach more people.

Your thoughts on how *The Grinning Gardener's Handbook Volume 3* helped you, what you liked most, or even areas where you'd like more information in future volumes, will help us create even better resources for gardeners like you.

How to Leave a Review:

1. Visit the book's page on Amazon.
2. Scroll down to the "Customer Reviews" section.
3. Click "Write a customer review" and share your thoughts!

Thank you for being part of our gardening community and for sharing your experience. Happy gardening!

The Grinning Gardener 🌿

CHAPTER 7
HARVESTING AND PRESERVING HERBS

There is a profound satisfaction in knowing that the herbs you've nurtured from tiny seedlings are now ready to be picked and used. This chapter focuses on recognizing when your herbs are at their peak for harvesting and how to do so in a way that ensures the health and longevity of your plants.

7.1 SIGNS YOUR HERBS ARE READY TO HARVEST

Understanding the growth stages of herbs is crucial for knowing the optimal time to harvest them. Leafy herbs, such as basil and mint, are best harvested before they flower. At this stage, the leaves are most tender and flavorful, containing the highest concentration of essential oils. Once these herbs begin to flower, they often divert their energy away from leaf production, causing the leaves to become bitter and less aromatic. By harvesting before flowering, you ensure that your herbs offer the best culinary experience.

Flowering herbs, like lavender and chamomile, are a different story. These herbs should be harvested when their flowers are at peak bloom but before they start to wilt. This timing ensures the highest concentration of essential oils, which are responsible for their fragrance and medicinal properties. The key is to monitor the flower buds closely and pick them just as they begin to open fully. Root herbs, such as ginger and turmeric, signal their readiness for harvest when the foliage begins to die back. As the leaves turn yellow and start to wither, the roots have reached their full size and flavor potential.

Specific signs of readiness can vary among different herbs. Basil, for example, should be harvested when the leaves are young and tender. These leaves are rich in essential oils and offer the best flavor for your dishes. Look for bright green leaves that are free of blemishes and feel slightly soft to the touch. Rosemary, on the other hand, is ready to be harvested when the stems are woody, and the foliage is fragrant. This usually occurs in the second year of growth. The leaves should be a deep green and emit a strong aroma when rubbed between your fingers. Mint, known for its vigorous growth, should be picked before the plant flowers. The leaves are most flavorful at this stage, offering a refreshing burst of minty goodness. Finally, chives are ready to be harvested when the stalks reach 6-8 inches tall. Snip the stalks close to the base, and they will regrow, allowing you to harvest multiple times throughout the season.

Timing your harvest can significantly impact the flavor and potency of your herbs. The best time of day to harvest is early in the morning, after the dew has dried but before the heat of the day sets in. During this time, the essential oils in the herbs are at their peak concentration, providing the richest flavor and aroma. Harvesting in the early morning also helps prevent wilting, as the cool temperatures and moisture levels are more favorable. Avoid harvesting during the midday heat, as the intense sun can cause the essential oils to evaporate, resulting in a loss of flavor and potency.

Maintaining plant health during harvest is essential to ensure continuous growth and productivity. Use sharp scissors or pruning shears to make clean cuts, minimizing damage to the plant. Dull tools can crush the stems, making it harder for the plant to heal and increasing the risk of disease. When harvesting, leave enough foliage on the plant to allow for regrowth. A good rule of thumb is to harvest no more than one-third of the plant at a time. This ensures that the plant retains enough leaves to continue photosynthesis and remain healthy. Rotating harvest areas is also crucial. Rather than stripping all the leaves from a single section, harvest a few leaves from different parts of the plant. This balanced approach helps the plant maintain its overall health and vigor.

Reflection Section: Harvesting Insights

- **Visual and Tactile Cues**: Make a note of how each herb looks and feels when it's ready to harvest. This will help you recognize the signs in the future.
- **Morning Routine**: Plan your harvesting schedule to take advantage of the early morning hours. Set a reminder to check your herbs daily during peak growing seasons.
- **Tool Care**: Keep your scissors and pruning shears sharp and clean. Regular maintenance ensures effective and healthy harvesting.

By understanding the growth stages of your herbs, recognizing specific signs of readiness, and timing your harvests correctly, you can ensure that your herbs retain their maximum flavor and potency. Proper harvesting techniques not only provide you with high-quality herbs but also contribute to the long-term health of your plants, allowing you to enjoy abundant harvests season after season.

7.2 TECHNIQUES FOR DRYING AND STORING HERBS

Drying herbs is a time-honored method to preserve their flavors and medicinal properties for extended use. One of the most straightforward and traditional techniques is air drying. This method involves tying herb stems into small bundles with twine and hanging them upside down in a well-ventilated area. A dark, dry spot, such as an attic or a pantry, is ideal to prevent the herbs from losing their color and potency. Ensure that the bundles are not too tight, allowing air to circulate freely around each stem. This process can take anywhere from a few days to a couple of weeks, depending on the humidity levels and the type of herb.

Once the leaves are crisp and crumble easily, they are sufficiently dried.

Oven drying is another effective method, particularly useful if you need to dry herbs quickly. Begin by spreading the herb leaves in a single layer on a baking sheet lined with parchment paper. Set your oven to its lowest temperature, typically around 100°F, and place the baking sheet inside. Keep the oven door slightly ajar to allow moisture to escape. Check the herbs every 15 minutes, turning them over to ensure even drying. This process usually takes about 30 minutes to an hour. Be cautious not to let the herbs become too dry, as this can cause them to lose their flavor and essential oils.

For those who prefer a more controlled and consistent drying process, using a food dehydrator is an excellent option. Dehydrators come with trays that allow you to spread the herbs in a single layer, ensuring even airflow around each leaf. Set the dehydrator to a low temperature, generally between 95°F and 115°F, and allow it to run for 2 to 4 hours, depending on the herb's moisture content. The advantage of a dehydrator is its ability to maintain a constant temperature and airflow, ensuring that the herbs dry evenly without the risk of mold or mildew.

Once your herbs are dried, proper storage is crucial to maintain their freshness and potency. The best way to store dried herbs is in airtight containers, such as glass jars or metal tins, which prevent moisture from getting in. Avoid using plastic bags, as they can trap moisture and lead to mold growth. Store these containers in a cool, dark place, away from direct sunlight and heat sources. Light and heat can degrade the herbs' essential oils, causing them to lose their flavor and medicinal properties. Label each container with the herb's name and the harvest date to keep track of their freshness. Properly stored, dried herbs can retain their quality for up to a year.

Common mistakes can compromise the quality of your dried herbs, so it's essential to be aware of them. One common pitfall is overcrowding the herbs during the drying process. When herbs are piled too closely together, air cannot circulate properly, leading to uneven drying and a higher risk of mold. Spread the herbs out as much as possible to ensure even airflow. Another mistake is storing herbs before they are fully dry. If any moisture remains, it can cause the entire batch to spoil. Always check that the herbs are brittle and crumble easily before storing them. Lastly, using plastic bags for storage is a no-go. Plastic can trap moisture, leading to mold and a loss of flavor. Always opt for airtight glass or metal containers to keep your herbs fresh and potent.

Drying and storing herbs properly ensures that you have a ready supply of flavorful and health beneficial herbs year-round. By understanding and applying these techniques, you can make the most of your herb harvests, preserving their qualities for future use. Whether you choose air drying, oven drying, or using a dehydrator, each method has its advantages and can be tailored to suit your preferences and needs.

7.3 FREEZING AND OTHER PRESERVATION METHODS

Freezing herbs is a fantastic way to maintain their fresh flavor and vibrant color, making it an ideal method for preserving herbs that you plan to use in cooking. While drying herbs concentrates their flavors, freezing retains a taste much closer to fresh herbs. This method is particularly useful for soft herbs like basil, cilantro, and parsley, which can lose their potency when dried. However, it's important to note that frozen herbs generally have a shorter shelf life compared to dried ones. They are best used within six months to a year for optimal flavor and quality.

The process of freezing herbs begins with selecting the freshest leaves. Start by washing the herbs thoroughly to remove any dirt or pests. Once cleaned, spread the leaves out on a baking sheet in a single layer. This step ensures that the leaves freeze individually rather than clumping together. Place the baking sheet in the freezer for a few hours until the leaves are fully frozen. Once frozen, transfer the leaves to a freezer bag or airtight container. This method works well for herbs like basil and mint, which retain their flavor and color when frozen quickly.

Another effective technique is freezing herbs in ice cube trays. This method is particularly useful for herbs that you plan to use in soups, stews, and sauces. Start by chopping the herbs finely and then spooning them into the compartments of an ice cube tray. Fill each compartment with water or olive oil to cover the herbs, then place the tray in the freezer. Once the cubes are frozen, transfer them to a freezer bag for long-term storage. This method not only preserves the herbs but also provides convenient portions that can be added directly to your cooking.

For those looking for a more advanced preservation method, vacuum sealing offers an excellent solution. This technique involves placing the herbs in a vacuum-seal bag and using a vacuum sealer to remove all the air before sealing the bag tightly. Vacuum sealing protects the herbs from freezer burn and extends their shelf life by minimizing exposure to air and moisture. This method is particularly effective for hardy herbs like rosemary and thyme, which can withstand the freezing process without losing their texture or flavor.

Beyond freezing, there are other creative ways to preserve herbs for culinary use. Herb butters are a delightful option, combining the fresh taste of herbs with the richness of butter. To make herb butter, chop your chosen herbs and mix them with softened butter. Shape the butter into a log, wrap it in parchment paper, and freeze. This herb-infused butter can be sliced as needed and used to enhance the flavor of dishes like roasted vegetables, grilled meats, or even a simple piece of toast.

Herb vinegars are another wonderful preservation method. Infusing vinegar with fresh herbs creates a flavorful condiment that can be used in salad dressings, marinades, and sauces. To make herb vinegar, place a handful of fresh herbs in a clean glass jar and cover them with your choice of vinegar, such as white wine or apple cider vinegar. Seal the jar tightly and store it in a cool, dark place for a few weeks, shaking it occasionally. Once the vinegar has absorbed the flavors, strain out the herbs and transfer the infused vinegar to a clean bottle.

Herb oils are a versatile and aromatic way to preserve the essence of fresh herbs. To make herb-infused oil, simply steep fresh herbs in olive oil. Wash and dry the herbs thoroughly to remove any moisture, then place them in a clean glass bottle and cover with olive oil. Seal the bottle and store it in a cool, dark place for a few weeks. This infusion process allows the oil to absorb the flavors and aromas of the herbs, resulting in a fragrant oil that can be used in cooking, drizzling over dishes, or as a dipping oil for bread.

Using frozen and preserved herbs in your cooking is both simple and rewarding. Frozen herbs can be added directly to soups, stews, and sauces without thawing. The heat of the cooking process will quickly rehydrate the herbs, releasing their flavors into the dish. Herb oils and vinegars can be used to create flavorful dressings and marinades, adding a burst of fresh herb taste to your meals. Herb butters are perfect for spreading on bread, melting over hot vegetables, or finishing a grilled steak. The convenience and versatility of these preserved herbs make them a valuable addition to any kitchen, ensuring you always have the fresh taste of herbs at your fingertips.

7.4 CREATING HERBAL INFUSIONS AND TINCTURES

Understanding the difference between infusions and tinctures is fundamental for anyone looking to make the most out of their homegrown herbs. Infusions are water-based extracts typically used for teas and culinary purposes. They are simple to prepare and offer a gentle way to enjoy the flavors and benefits of herbs. Tinctures, on the other hand, are alcohol-based extracts used primarily for health purposes. They concentrate the active ingredients of herbs, making them potent remedies for various ailments.

To make an herbal infusion, start by selecting your herbs. Both fresh and dried herbs can be used, but dried herbs often have a more concentrated flavor. Measure the herbs to ensure optimal strength—generally, one tablespoon of dried herb or two tablespoons of fresh herb per cup of water. Bring water to a boil, then pour it over the herbs. Cover the container to trap the steam and essential oils, letting it steep for the required time. Most leaf-based infusions are ready in 10-15 minutes, while root-based infusions may require longer steeping times to extract their beneficial compounds. Once steeped, strain the herbs and enjoy your infusion.

Creating tinctures involves a bit more preparation but yields a powerful and long-lasting extract. Begin by choosing a high-proof alcohol like vodka or brandy, which acts as a solvent to extract the health properties from the herbs. Chop your fresh or dried herbs finely and place them in a clean glass jar. Pour the alcohol over the herbs, ensuring they are fully submerged. Seal the jar tightly and store it in a cool, dark place. Shake the jar daily to mix the contents and aid the extraction process. After a few weeks, usually around six to eight, strain the mixture through a fine mesh strainer or cheesecloth. Transfer the liquid to dark glass bottles for storage, as exposure to light can degrade the tincture's potency.

Using herbal infusions and tinctures requires careful attention to dosage and application. For infusions, a cup or two a day is typically safe for most people. They can be enjoyed as a soothing tea or added to culinary dishes for a burst of herbal flavor. Tinctures, being more concentrated, should be used with caution. A common dosage is 1-2 milliliters, or about 30-60 drops, diluted in water or juice. It's essential to start with a lower dose and gradually increase as needed, always consulting with a healthcare provider for holistic health use to avoid any adverse effects or interactions with other medications.

Incorporating these herbal preparations into your daily routine can enhance both your culinary experiences and your wellbeing. Herbal infusions offer a gentle way to enjoy the flavors and benefits of your garden, while tinctures provide a potent remedy for various health concerns. By mastering these techniques, you can fully utilize the herbs you grow, ensuring they contribute to a healthier, more flavorful life.

Infusions and tinctures are just two ways to make the most of your herb garden. They offer versatility in how you can enjoy and benefit from the plants you nurture. Whether you seek the soothing comfort of an herbal tea or the potent effects of a medicinal tincture, these methods open up a world of possibilities. By understanding and applying these techniques, you can create a more holistic and rewarding herb gardening experience.

CHAPTER 8
CULINARY USES OF HERBS

H erbs have a unique way of elevating dishes, adding complexity and depth that turn ordinary recipes into culinary masterpieces. This chapter will explore the essential culinary herbs you should consider growing, their unique flavor profiles, and how best to use them in your cooking.

8.1 ESSENTIAL CULINARY HERBS AND THEIR USES

Basil

Basil is a must-have in any herb garden, known for its sweet and aromatic flavor that is a cornerstone of Italian cuisine. Its leaves carry a slight pepperiness with hints of anise, making it perfect for a variety of dishes. Think of a classic pesto, where basil's vibrant flavor melds beautifully with pine nuts, garlic, Parmesan, and olive oil. A caprese salad, with fresh basil, ripe tomatoes, and mozzarella, becomes a symphony of summer flavors. Basil also shines in a simple tomato sauce, where its sweetness balances the acidity of the tomatoes. To keep basil fresh, treat it like a bouquet of flowers: place the stems in a jar of water and store it on your kitchen counter. This not only keeps the leaves vibrant but also adds a lovely green touch to your kitchen decor.

Thyme

Thyme is another essential herb, offering a subtle, earthy flavor with a hint of mint. Its versatility makes it a staple in many kitchens. Thyme is particularly well-suited for roasting meats, where its robust flavor can stand up to the heat. Picture a roasted chicken, seasoned with thyme, garlic, and lemon, filling your home with an irresistible aroma. Thyme also enhances the depth of soups and stews, adding a layer of complexity that transforms simple ingredients into hearty, comforting meals. To store thyme, wrap it in a damp paper towel and place it in a resealable plastic bag in the refrigerator. This method helps retain its moisture and flavor for longer periods.

Cilantro

Cilantro, with its fresh and citrusy notes, is indispensable in Mexican and Asian cuisines. Its bright, slightly spicy flavor can bring a dish to life. Imagine a zesty salsa, where cilantro's sharpness cuts through the richness of tomatoes and onions. In guacamole, it adds a refreshing contrast to the creamy avocado. Cilantro also works wonders in pho, the aromatic Vietnamese soup, where it complements the broth's complex flavors. To freeze cilantro, chop it finely and place it in ice cube trays with a little water or oil. Once frozen, transfer the cubes to a freezer bag, and you'll have fresh cilantro ready to use anytime.

Dill

Dill, with its light and feathery fronds, offers a fresh, tangy, and slightly grassy flavor. It's a natural partner for pickling, where its distinct taste permeates the brine, creating classic dill pickles. Dill also pairs beautifully with seafood, enhancing dishes like gravlax with its bright, herbaceous notes. A simple potato salad, tossed with fresh dill, yogurt, and garlic, becomes a refreshing side dish perfect for summer picnics. To keep dill fresh, store it in a plastic bag with a damp paper towel in the refrigerator. This helps maintain its delicate texture and vibrant flavor.

These essential culinary herbs not only enhance the flavors of your dishes but also bring a touch of freshness and vitality to your cooking. By understanding their unique characteristics and best uses, you can elevate your meals and enjoy the full spectrum of flavors they offer. Whether you're making a simple salad or a complex stew, these herbs are your allies in creating delicious, memorable dishes that celebrate the bounty of your garden.

8.2 HERB PAIRINGS FOR ENHANCED FLAVORS

Understanding the concept of herb pairings can transform your cooking. Combining herbs creates complex and harmonious flavors that elevate your dishes. Think of it as a symphony, where each herb plays a unique role while complementing the others. Complementary flavors are key. Strong herbs like rosemary can be balanced by milder ones like thyme. This balance ensures that no single herb overwhelms the dish but rather, they work together to create a nuanced flavor profile.

Classic herb pairings have stood the test of time for a reason. Consider basil and oregano, a duo that brings out the best in Italian dishes. Whether you're making a classic marinara sauce or a simple margherita pizza, these two herbs harmonize beautifully, offering a blend of sweetness and earthiness. Rosemary and thyme are another timeless pairing, perfect for roasted meats and vegetables. The robust, piney notes of rosemary complement the subtle mintiness of thyme, creating a well-rounded flavor that enhances the dish's natural taste.

Experimenting with new pairings can be an exciting culinary adventure. Start with a flavor wheel to identify complementary herbs. This tool helps you see which herbs share similar flavor profiles and can work well together. Testing small amounts of new pairings in simple dishes allows you to gauge how they interact without overwhelming your palate. Keep a journal of successful combinations. Note the herbs used, the dish they enhanced, and any tweaks you made. This record becomes a valuable resource, guiding your future culinary experiments.

Herbs play distinct roles in different cuisines. In Mediterranean cooking, basil, oregano, and rosemary are staples. They bring a taste of the sun-drenched coastlines to your table, enhancing dishes like pasta, roasted vegetables, and grilled meats. Asian cuisine often features cilantro, mint, and Thai basil. These herbs add brightness and complexity to dishes such as spring rolls, curries, and noodle salads. Middle Eastern cuisine frequently uses parsley, mint, and dill, herbs that infuse dishes like tabbouleh, falafel, and yogurt sauces with fresh, vibrant flavors.

Using these principles, you can start to see herbs not just as individual ingredients but as part of a larger palette. Just as an artist mixes colors to achieve the perfect shade, you can combine herbs to create flavors that are greater than the sum of their parts. This approach opens up endless possibilities for your cooking, allowing you to experiment and discover new favorites. Whether you're sticking to classic combinations or venturing into new territory, understanding herb pairings will enrich your culinary experience.

8.3 RECIPES FEATURING FRESH HERBS

One of my favorite ways to celebrate the flavors of fresh herbs is through cooking. There's something magical about how a handful of fresh basil can transform a simple dish into something extraordinary.

Basil Pesto

Let's start with a classic: basil pesto. This vibrant green sauce not only highlights the sweet and aromatic notes of basil but also brings together the richness of pine nuts and Parmesan cheese. To prepare, you'll need two cups of fresh basil leaves, one-third cup of pine nuts, three cloves of garlic, half a cup of grated Parmesan, and half a cup of olive oil. Blend the basil, pine nuts, and garlic in a food processor until finely chopped. Gradually add the Parmesan and olive oil, blending until smooth. This pesto can be tossed with pasta, spread on sandwiches, or used as a dip. For those with nut allergies or seeking a different flavor profile, walnuts make a great substitute for pine nuts, adding a slightly earthier taste.

Herb-Crusted Chicken

Another fantastic recipe that showcases fresh herbs is herb-crusted chicken. This dish combines the robust flavors of thyme, rosemary, and parsley to create a savory crust that infuses the chicken with aromatic goodness. Start with four boneless, skinless chicken breasts. Mix two tablespoons each of chopped fresh thyme, rosemary, and parsley with two cloves of minced garlic, one teaspoon of salt, and half a teaspoon of black pepper. Rub this mixture evenly over the chicken breasts. Preheat your oven to 375°F. Heat two tablespoons of olive oil in an oven-safe skillet over medium-high heat and sear the chicken for two to three minutes on each side until golden. Transfer the skillet to the oven and bake for 20 minutes or until the chicken is cooked through. Serve with roasted vegetables or a fresh salad for a complete meal. If you prefer a lighter taste, consider using lemon zest in place of garlic to add a citrusy brightness.

Cilantro-Lime Rice

For a side dish that's bursting with fresh, zesty flavors, cilantro-lime rice is a must-try. This dish pairs beautifully with Mexican and Asian cuisines, adding a refreshing twist to your meals. Begin by cooking one cup of long-grain white rice according to the package instructions. Once cooked, fluff the rice with a fork and stir in the juice of one lime, one cup of chopped fresh cilantro, and two tablespoons of olive oil. Season with salt and pepper to taste. For a variation, you can substitute parsley for cilantro if you're looking for a different flavor profile. This rice makes an excellent base for burrito bowls, pairs well with grilled fish, or serves as a fresh side for tacos.

Dill and Cucumber Salad

Dill and cucumber salad is another delightful recipe that highlights the light and feathery fronds of fresh dill. This salad is cool and crisp, making it perfect for hot summer days. Slice two large cucumbers into thin rounds and place them in a bowl. In a separate bowl, mix half a cup of Greek yogurt, two tablespoons of chopped fresh dill, one clove of minced garlic, and the juice of half a lemon. Season with salt and pepper to taste. Pour the yogurt mixture over the cucumbers and toss to coat. For added freshness, you can sprinkle in some chopped mint leaves. This salad is a fantastic side dish for grilled meats or can be enjoyed on its own as a refreshing snack.

Cooking with fresh herbs not only enhances the flavor of your dishes but also offers numerous health benefits. Basil is rich in antioxidants, which help combat oxidative stress in the body. Thyme has anti-inflammatory properties that can help reduce inflammation and support overall health. Cilantro aids in digestion and is known for its detoxifying properties. Dill, with its immune-boosting effects, can help support your body's natural defenses. By incorporating these herbs into your cooking, you're not just making your meals more delicious—you're also nourishing your body with essential nutrients and health-promoting compounds.

8.4 MAKING HERB-INFUSED OILS AND VINEGARS

Herb-infused oils and vinegars are culinary wonders that can add depth and complexity to your dishes. Imagine drizzling a rich rosemary-infused olive oil over roasted vegetables, instantly elevating their flavor, or using a basil-infused vinegar to create a vibrant salad dressing that makes every bite a delight. These infusions can turn everyday meals into gourmet experiences, making them a must-have in your kitchen arsenal. They not only enhance the taste of salads and marinades but also bring a touch of sophistication to your cooking, allowing you to experiment with flavors and create unique culinary masterpieces.

Creating your own herb-infused oils is a rewarding process that starts with selecting high-quality olive oil or another oil of your choice, such as grapeseed or sunflower oil. Fresh herbs like rosemary, thyme, or basil are ideal for infusions due to their robust flavors. Begin by washing and thoroughly drying the herbs to remove any dirt or moisture, which can cause spoilage. Next, gently heat the oil in a saucepan over low heat until it reaches about 140°F. Add the herbs to the oil, ensuring they are fully submerged, and let them simmer for about 5-10 minutes to release their flavors. Be careful not to overheat the oil, as this can damage the delicate flavors of the herbs. Once the infusion is complete, strain the oil through a fine mesh sieve or cheesecloth to remove the herb solids. Pour the strained oil into sterilized bottles and seal them tightly. Store the infused oil in a cool, dark place to preserve its freshness and flavor.

Creating herb-infused vinegars follows a similar process but uses a different base. Choose a high-quality vinegar such as white wine, apple cider, or balsamic vinegar, each offering a unique flavor profile that complements different herbs. For example, tarragon pairs wonderfully with white wine vinegar, while dill and basil can add a refreshing twist to apple cider vinegar. Start by washing and drying the herbs, then lightly bruise them to release their essential oils. Place the herbs in a sterilized glass jar and pour the vinegar over them, ensuring the herbs are fully submerged. Seal the jar tightly and store it in a cool, dark place for at least two weeks, shaking it gently every few days to help the flavors meld. After the infusion period, strain the vinegar through a fine mesh sieve or cheesecloth to remove the herb solids. Pour the strained vinegar into sterilized bottles and seal them tightly. These infused vinegars can be stored in the refrigerator to maintain their freshness and vibrant flavors.

Herb-infused oils and vinegars are incredibly versatile and can be used in a myriad of ways to enhance your cooking. Drizzle rosemary-infused oil over roasted vegetables like potatoes, carrots, and Brussels sprouts for an added layer of flavor. Use basil-infused vinegar to create a zesty salad dressing by mixing it with olive oil, Dijon mustard, and a touch of honey. Marinating meats with herb-infused oils not only adds flavor but also helps tenderize the meat, making it more succulent and delicious. Try marinating chicken breasts in a mixture of thyme-infused oil, garlic, and lemon juice for a simple yet flavorful dish. Herb-infused vinegars can also be added to sauces and reductions to provide a burst of acidity and complexity. A splash of tarragon-infused vinegar in a béarnaise sauce can elevate a steak to new heights, while dill-infused vinegar can bring a refreshing tang to a creamy cucumber salad.

By making your own herb-infused oils and vinegars, you not only enhance the flavors of your dishes but also gain the satisfaction of creating something unique and personal. These infusions allow you to capture the essence of fresh herbs and enjoy their vibrant flavors year-round. Experiment with different combinations and discover your own favorite pairings, adding a touch of gourmet flair to your everyday cooking.

In the next chapter, we will explore the holistic health uses of herbs, delving into how these powerful plants can support your health and well-being. From teas to tinctures, you'll learn how to harness the healing properties of your garden's bounty.

CHAPTER 9
HOLISTIC HEALTH USES
OF HERBS

This chapter will introduce you to some of the most widely used holistic health herbs and how they can benefit your health.

9.1 COMMON HOLISTIC HEALTH HERBS AND THEIR BENEFITS

Chamomile

Chamomile is one of the most ancient holistic health herbs known to humankind. Revered for its calming and anti-inflammatory properties, chamomile is a go-to remedy for reducing anxiety and promoting sleep. The herb contains apigenin, a natural sedative that binds to receptors in your brain, helping to initiate sleep and reduce anxiety. Chamomile tea is a popular way to consume this herb. Drinking a cup before bed can help you unwind and prepare for a restful night. Additionally, chamomile has been shown to alleviate symptoms of gastrointestinal disorders, making it a versatile herb for your medicinal herb garden.

Echinacea

Echinacea is another powerhouse in the world of medicinal herbs. Known for its immune-boosting and antiviral properties, echinacea is commonly used to help prevent the common cold. The herb is rich in alkylamides and polysaccharides, which stimulate the immune system and enhance your body's ability to fight off infections. Echinacea can be consumed as a tincture during the cold season to bolster your immunity. Its antiviral properties have also been shown to be effective against respiratory viruses, making it a valuable addition to your herbal medicine cabinet.

Lavender

Lavender is celebrated for its relaxing and antiseptic qualities. High in linalool and linalyl acetate, lavender is effective in alleviating stress and soothing skin irritations. The herb's calming scent can help reduce anxiety and improve sleep quality. Adding a few drops of lavender oil to a bath or diffuser can create a relaxing atmosphere, perfect for unwinding after a long day. Lavender's antiseptic properties also make it useful for treating minor cuts and burns. Applying a diluted lavender oil to the affected area can help speed up the healing process and prevent infections.

Peppermint

Peppermint is a versatile herb known for its digestive aid and pain-relieving properties. Containing menthol and menthone, peppermint can help relieve indigestion and headaches. Drinking peppermint tea after meals can ease digestive symptoms like gas, bloating, and indigestion. The herb's muscle relaxant properties also make it effective in alleviating tension headaches. Applying peppermint oil to the temples can provide quick relief from headache pain. Additionally, peppermint's antibacterial properties can help freshen breath and support oral health.

Incorporating these holistic health herbs into your daily routine can offer numerous benefits. Chamomile tea is a simple and effective way to reduce anxiety and promote sleep. Echinacea tinctures can be taken during the cold season to enhance your immune defenses. Lavender oil can be added to baths or diffusers to create a calming environment, while peppermint tea can be sipped after meals to aid digestion and relieve headaches.

Understanding the active compounds in these herbs is essential for appreciating their therapeutic effects. Chamomile's bioactive constituents, such as volatile oils, terpenoids, and flavonoids, contribute to its health benefits. Echinacea's antiviral activities are attributed to its polyphenols, alkylamides, and other bioactive compounds. Lavender's high content of linalool and linalyl acetate is responsible for its calming and antiseptic properties. Peppermint's menthol and menthone provide its digestive and pain-relieving effects.

By growing these holistic health herbs in your garden, you can harness their therapeutic properties and incorporate them into your daily life. Whether you are drinking chamomile tea to unwind, taking echinacea tincture to boost your immune system, adding lavender oil to your bath for relaxation, or sipping peppermint tea after meals to aid digestion, these herbs offer a natural and effective way to support your health. The next subchapter will delve into more practical tips and detailed uses for these and other holistic health herbs.

9.2 PREPARING HERBAL TEAS AND DECOCTIONS

Herbal teas and decoctions are two distinct methods of extracting the beneficial compounds from herbs. Understanding the difference between these preparations can help you choose the right method for your needs. Herbal teas, also known as infusions, are made by steeping the delicate parts of the plant, such as leaves and flowers, in hot water. This gentle method preserves the volatile oils and aromatic compounds that contribute to the herb's therapeutic effects. In contrast, decoctions involve simmering the tougher parts of the plant, like roots and bark, to extract their more robust and resilient compounds. This method is ideal for herbs that require more intensive processing to release their health properties.

Making herbal teas is a straightforward process that begins with selecting either fresh or dried herbs. Fresh herbs are often preferred for their vibrant flavors and potent health qualities, but dried herbs can also be effective and are more convenient to store. Measure out the appropriate amount of herbs, typically 1-2 teaspoons per cup of water, and place them in a teapot or a heat-proof container. Pour boiling water over the herbs, ensuring they are fully submerged. Allow the herbs to steep for 5-10 minutes, depending on the desired strength. After steeping, strain the tea to remove the plant material, and your herbal infusion is ready to enjoy. This method is perfect for preparing calming chamomile tea, which can help you unwind after a long day.

For a more concentrated herbal preparation, decoctions are the way to go. Begin by choosing the right herbs for this method, such as ginger or licorice root, which require longer simmering to release their medicinal compounds. Measure out the herbs and add them to a pot with cold water. Use about 1-2 tablespoons of dried roots or bark per cup of water. Bring the mixture to a boil, then reduce the heat and let it simmer for 20-30 minutes. The extended simmering time allows the tough plant materials to break down and release their therapeutic compounds into the water. After simmering, strain the liquid to remove the plant material, and consume the decoction while it is still warm. Ginger decoction is particularly beneficial as an anti-inflammatory and digestive aid, making it a valuable addition to your wellness routine.

Herbal teas and decoctions offer specific therapeutic benefits depending on the herbs used. Chamomile tea, for instance, is well-known for its calming and sleep-inducing properties. The gentle infusion method preserves chamomile's volatile oils and flavonoids, which help to soothe the nervous system and promote relaxation. Ginger decoction, on the other hand, is highly effective for reducing inflammation and aiding digestion. The robust simmering process extracts ginger's anti-inflammatory compounds, making it a powerful remedy for digestive discomfort and joint pain. Echinacea tea is another excellent option, particularly for immune support. The infusion method extracts echinacea's polysaccharides and alkylamides, which enhance immune function and help the body fight off infections. Licorice root decoction is soothing for sore throats and respiratory issues. The extended simmering releases glycyrrhizin, a compound known for its anti-inflammatory and antimicrobial properties, providing relief from throat irritation and promoting respiratory health.

Incorporating these herbal preparations into your daily routine can offer numerous health benefits. For instance, sipping chamomile tea before bed can help you relax and improve your sleep quality. Drinking a cup of ginger decoction in the morning can kickstart your digestion and reduce inflammation throughout the day. Echinacea tea can be consumed during the cold season to boost your immune system and ward off infections. Licorice root decoction can be particularly soothing during the winter months when sore throats and respiratory issues are more common. By understanding the methods and benefits of herbal teas and decoctions, you can harness the healing power of herbs in a way that fits seamlessly into your lifestyle.

9.3 MAKING SALVES, BALMS, AND LOTIONS

Creating your own topical herbal preparations can be incredibly rewarding. Salves, balms, and lotions are three common types of these preparations, each with its unique consistency and use. Salves are oil-based and have a thicker consistency, making them ideal for healing and protecting the skin. They are excellent for treating minor cuts, burns, and dry patches. Balms are like salves but are firmer, often used for lip care or targeted treatments like muscle relief. Lotions, on the other hand, are emulsions of water and oil, designed to moisturize and nourish the skin while being lighter and more easily absorbed.

To make a herbal salve, start by infusing a carrier oil with your chosen herbs, such as calendula or comfrey. These herbs are well-known for their skin-healing properties. Place the dried herbs in a jar and cover them with a carrier oil like olive or almond oil. Let the mixture sit in a warm, sunny spot for a few weeks to allow the herbs to infuse their beneficial compounds into the oil. After the infusion period, strain the oil to remove the herb material. Next, melt beeswax in a double boiler and mix it with the infused oil. The beeswax will give the salve its thick consistency and help it solidify. Pour the mixture into clean containers and let it cool completely before use. This salve can be applied to dry or irritated skin to promote healing and provide relief.

Creating herbal balms is a similar process, but with slight variations to achieve the desired firmness. For a soothing lip balm, infuse oil with calendula, which is known for its gentle and healing properties. Strain the infused oil and melt it with beeswax and a small amount of coconut oil in a double boiler. The coconut oil adds extra moisturizing benefits and a pleasant texture. Pour the mixture into small lip balm tubes or tins and let it cool. For a muscle balm, use arnica and peppermint oil, which are effective for pain relief and reducing inflammation. Infuse the arnica in a carrier oil, strain, and combine with beeswax and a few drops of peppermint essential oil. Pour into containers and let it set. This muscle balm can be massaged into sore muscles to alleviate pain and promote relaxation.

Making herbal lotions involves blending infused oils with water and an emulsifying wax to create a smooth and creamy texture. Start by infusing your chosen herbs in a carrier oil, such as calendula for its moisturizing properties. Strain the oil and heat it gently with emulsifying wax until melted. In a separate pot, heat distilled water until warm. Slowly pour the warm water into the oil and wax mixture while blending with a hand mixer or immersion blender. Continue blending until the mixture emulsifies and becomes smooth. Add a few drops of essential oils, such as lavender for its calming effects, and blend again. Pour the lotion into sterilized containers and let it cool completely. A calendula lotion is excellent for dry skin, providing deep hydration and soothing irritation. A lavender lotion can be used to relax and soothe sensitive skin before bedtime.

Creating these herbal preparations allows you to customize your skincare routine with natural, effective ingredients. Salves provide healing and protection, balms offer targeted relief, and lotions deliver moisture and nourishment. By infusing oils with beneficial herbs and combining them with beeswax, coconut oil, and essential oils, you can create a range of products tailored to your needs. Whether you're treating dry skin, soothing sore muscles, or simply

enjoying the calming effects of lavender, these homemade preparations bring the power of herbs into your daily self-care routine.

9.4 SAFETY AND DOSAGE GUIDELINES FOR HOLISTIC HEALTH HERBS

Understanding the correct dosage of holistic health herbs is
crucial for ensuring their safety and effectiveness. Just like conven-
tional medications, herbs have active compounds that can cause
side effects if not used properly. Proper dosage helps prevent
potential adverse reactions and ensures you get the therapeutic
benefits you seek. For instance, consuming too much chamomile
tea can lead to drowsiness, while excessive use of peppermint oil
might cause skin irritation. By adhering to recommended dosages,
you can enjoy the health benefits of these herbs while minimizing
the risk of side effects.

For chamomile tea, drinking 1-2 cups per day is generally considered safe and effective. This amount helps to reduce anxiety and
promote restful sleep without causing undue sedation. Echinacea
tincture, often used to boost the immune system, is typically taken
in doses of 2-3 ml up to three times a day. This dosage helps
enhance your body's defenses against colds and other infections.
Lavender oil, known for its calming and antiseptic properties, can
be used in a diffuser with 2-3 drops or applied topically when
diluted. This provides a soothing environment and aids in
relieving stress. Peppermint tea, beneficial for digestion and
headache relief, is best consumed in quantities of 1-2 cups per day
to avoid potential gastric irritation.

It's essential to be aware of potential side effects and contraindica-
tions when using herbs for holistic health purposes. Chamomile,
for example, can cause allergic reactions in individuals sensitive to
ragweed, as it belongs to the same plant family. If you have a
known allergy to ragweed, it's advisable to avoid chamomile or

consult with a healthcare provider before use. Echinacea should be used with caution in individuals with autoimmune conditions, as it can stimulate the immune system and potentially exacerbate these conditions. Lavender oil should be used cautiously during pregnancy, as its effects on fetal development are not fully understood. Peppermint may aggravate acid reflux in some people, so those with gastroesophageal reflux disease (GERD) should use it sparingly.

Consulting with healthcare professionals before incorporating herbs into your routine for holistic health is always a good practice. Discussing herbal use with a doctor or naturopath can help you understand how these herbs might interact with any medications you're currently taking. For instance, some herbs can affect blood clotting, which is crucial information if you're on blood thinners. Healthcare professionals can also provide personalized recommendations based on your health history and current conditions, ensuring that you use herbs as a complementary treatment rather than a primary one.

By understanding the importance of proper dosage, being aware of potential side effects, and seeking professional advice, you can safely incorporate holistic health herbs into your daily life. These guidelines help you make informed decisions, allowing you to harness the therapeutic benefits of herbs while minimizing risks. In the next chapter, we will explore how to grow herbs indoors and in small spaces, ensuring that even those with limited outdoor areas can enjoy the benefits of a thriving herb garden.

CHAPTER 10
INDOOR AND SMALL
SPACE HERB GARDENING

This chapter will guide you through the practicalities of growing herbs indoors, even in the smallest of spaces, ensuring you have a continuous supply of fresh, flavorful, and medicinally potent plants.

10.1 CHOOSING CONTAINERS AND POTS FOR INDOOR HERBS

Selecting the right containers for your indoor herb garden is a crucial step that can significantly impact the health and growth of your plants. The containers you choose must provide proper drainage to prevent root rot, a common issue in indoor gardening where excess water can suffocate roots. Without adequate drainage, herbs can quickly become waterlogged, leading to the decay of their roots and eventually the plant's demise. Look for pots with drainage holes at the bottom, and if you find a container you love without them, consider drilling your own.

Another important factor to consider is the size of the containers. Each herb has its own space requirements, and choosing a pot that matches the mature size of the plant is essential. For instance, a small pot may be sufficient for herbs like thyme or oregano, which have shallow root systems. However, larger herbs like rosemary or basil will require more substantial containers to accommodate their extensive root networks. Ensuring that your herbs have enough room to grow will not only promote healthy development but also prevent the plants from becoming root-bound, which can stunt growth and reduce vitality.

There are various types of containers to choose from, each with its own advantages and disadvantages. Terracotta pots are a popular choice due to their porosity, which allows for good airflow to the roots. This characteristic is particularly beneficial for herbs that prefer drier soil, as it helps to prevent water from accumulating around the roots. However, terracotta pots can dry out quickly, so you'll need to monitor soil moisture levels regularly. Plastic pots, on the other hand, are lightweight and retain moisture well, making them ideal for herbs that require consistently moist soil. They are also typically less expensive and come in a variety of shapes and sizes.

Fabric pots are another excellent option for indoor gardening. These breathable containers promote healthy root growth by allowing air to penetrate the soil, which helps prevent root rot and encourages a more robust root system. Additionally, fabric pots are lightweight and easy to move, making them a versatile choice for indoor gardeners. Self-watering containers are particularly useful for those who may not have the time to water their plants regularly. These pots have a built-in reservoir that provides a steady supply of water to the plant, reducing the risk of over or under-watering and ensuring your herbs remain healthy and hydrated.

For those who enjoy a touch of creativity and sustainability in their gardening practices, repurposing household items as containers can be both fun and environmentally friendly. Mason jars, for example, can be transformed into charming herb planters by adding a layer of pebbles or gravel at the bottom for drainage. Tin cans, once cleaned and with drainage holes punched into the bottom, can make quirky, rustic pots for your herbs. Wooden boxes can also be repurposed into planters, providing a natural and aesthetically pleasing option for your indoor garden. These DIY containers not only add a personal touch to your space but also promote sustainable gardening practices by reusing materials that might otherwise be discarded.

When setting up your indoor herb garden, don't overlook the importance of container accessories. Saucer trays placed under pots will catch any excess water that drains out, protecting your windowsills and countertops from water damage. Pebble trays can also be beneficial, especially in dry indoor environments. By placing a layer of pebbles in a tray and adding water, you create a humid microclimate around your plants as the water evaporates. This added humidity can be particularly beneficial for herbs like basil and mint, which thrive in moist conditions. Plant stands are another useful accessory, allowing you to elevate and display your herbs while ensuring they receive adequate light and airflow.

By carefully selecting the right containers and accessories for your indoor herb garden, you create an environment where your plants can thrive. This thoughtful approach not only ensures the health and vitality of your herbs but also enhances the beauty and functionality of your indoor space. Whether you choose traditional terracotta pots, modern self-watering containers, or repurposed household items, the key is to provide the right conditions for your herbs to flourish.

10.2 VERTICAL GARDENING AND HERB SPIRALS

In the confines of small apartments and urban settings, vertical gardening becomes a practical and innovative solution. By utilizing vertical space, you can grow a variety of herbs without requiring a large footprint. This method is especially beneficial when floor space is limited, allowing you to create a lush, green environment even in the most compact areas.

There are numerous design ideas to explore when venturing into vertical gardening. Wall-mounted planters are an excellent way to transform bare walls into productive green spaces. These planters can be arranged in patterns, creating an aesthetic appeal while providing ample room for your herbs to grow. Hanging baskets and pocket planters offer another creative solution, suspending your herbs in mid-air and making use of overhead space. Trellises and lattice structures can support climbing herbs like mint and oregano, encouraging upward growth and maximizing the use of vertical space. DIY pallet gardens are a popular and budget-friendly option, where old wooden pallets are repurposed into vertical planters. Simply attach pots or plant directly into the pallet slats, and you have a rustic yet functional garden.

Herb spirals present a unique and efficient way to maximize space while creating a microclimate that caters to the diverse needs of different herbs. Imagine a spiral-shaped bed, constructed with rocks or bricks, where herbs are planted in a cascading pattern. This design takes advantage of gravity and varying sun exposure, allowing you to place sun-loving herbs like rosemary and thyme at the top, where they receive the most light. Herbs that prefer more moisture, such as mint and chives, are planted at the bottom, where water naturally collects. The spiral structure not only saves space but also creates different microenvironments within a small area, making it possible to grow a variety of herbs with differing requirements.

Building an herb spiral is a rewarding project that can be completed with a few simple steps. First, select a suitable location that receives at least six hours of sunlight daily. The placement of your spiral is crucial, as it determines the success of your herbs. Once you've chosen the location, gather your materials, including bricks, stones, soil, and compost. Start by laying a base of rocks or gravel to improve drainage. Next, build the spiral structure by stacking bricks or stones in a circular pattern, starting from the center and gradually decreasing the height as you move outward. Fill the spiral with a mixture of soil and compost, layering it to ensure even distribution of nutrients.

When planting your herbs, consider their light and water needs. Place sun-loving herbs like rosemary and lavender at the top, where they will thrive in full sunlight. Herbs that require more moisture, such as parsley and cilantro, should be planted closer to the bottom. The middle sections can be reserved for herbs with moderate water and light requirements, like basil and oregano. As you plant, make sure to space the herbs appropriately to allow for adequate airflow and growth. Water the spiral thoroughly after planting to help the soil settle and the roots establish.

An herb spiral not only provides a functional and space-efficient gardening solution but also adds an attractive focal point to your garden. The varying heights and textures of the plants create visual interest, while the spiral design allows for easy access to all your herbs. This method is particularly useful for urban gardeners looking to maximize limited space and create a productive, thriving garden.

Vertical gardening and herb spirals offer creative and practical ways to grow herbs in small spaces. Whether you choose to build a vertical garden with wall-mounted planters, hanging baskets, or trellises, or opt for the unique design of an herb spiral, these methods will help you make the most of your available space. Embrace the possibilities of vertical gardening and enjoy a bountiful harvest of fresh, flavorful herbs right at your fingertips.

10.3 HYDROPONIC AND AEROPONIC HERB GARDENING

Hydroponic gardening offers a fascinating way to grow herbs without soil, using nutrient-rich water solutions. The benefits of hydroponics are numerous, making it an attractive option for indoor gardening. By eliminating soil, you reduce the risk of soil-borne diseases that can plague traditional gardens. This method also tends to produce faster growth rates and higher yields because the plants receive a constant supply of nutrients directly to their roots. The controlled environment of hydroponics ensures that your herbs get exactly what they need, resulting in robust and healthy plants.

There are several types of hydroponic systems you can choose from, each with its own set of advantages. Deep Water Culture (DWC) is one of the simplest systems, where the roots of the plants are suspended in a nutrient solution. An air pump provides oxygen to the roots, promoting healthy growth. The Nutrient Film Technique (NFT) involves a thin film of nutrient solution flowing over the roots, which are supported in a trough or channel. This method is efficient and conserves water. Wick systems are another option, where a wick draws the nutrient solution from a reservoir into the growing medium. This passive system requires no pumps, making it easy to set up and maintain. The Ebb and Flow system, also known as Flood and Drain, periodically floods the grow bed with nutrient solution before draining it back into a reservoir. This method ensures that the roots receive both nutrients and oxygen, mimicking natural wet and dry cycles.

Setting up a hydroponic system requires some initial planning and investment. You can either purchase a ready-made hydroponic kit or build your own DIY system. When selecting a system, consider the space you have available and the types of herbs you wish to grow. Nutrient selection is crucial, as hydroponic plants rely entirely on the nutrients provided in the solution. Choose a balanced hydroponic nutrient formula and monitor the pH levels to ensure they stay within the optimal range of 5.5 to 6.5. Water temperature and oxygen levels are also important factors. The ideal temperature for hydroponic systems is between 65-75°F. Use an air pump to oxygenate the water, preventing root rot and promoting healthy growth. Regularly check the nutrient concentration to make sure your plants are getting the right amount of nourishment.

Aeroponic gardening takes the concept of soil-less growing to another level by suspending the plant roots in the air and misting them with nutrient solutions. This method offers several advantages, including increased oxygenation to the roots, which can lead to faster growth and greater yields. The roots are exposed to more oxygen, which enhances nutrient absorption and overall plant health. Aeroponics also reduces the risk of root diseases, as the roots are not constantly submerged in water.

To set up an aeroponic system, you can choose between an aeroponic tower or a DIY setup. An aeroponic tower is a vertical system that uses a pump to mist the roots with nutrient solution at regular intervals. This setup is space-efficient and ideal for small indoor gardens. When building a DIY aeroponic system, you'll need a container to hold the nutrient solution, a pump, misting nozzles, and a timer to control the misting intervals. Proper misting intervals are crucial for the success of an aeroponic system. The roots should be misted for a few seconds every few minutes to ensure they stay moist but not waterlogged. Adequate lighting and air circulation are also essential. Use grow lights to provide the necessary light spectrum and ensure good airflow to prevent mold and mildew.

Both hydroponic and aeroponic systems offer innovative ways to grow herbs indoors, each with its unique benefits. Whether you opt for the simplicity of a hydroponic system or the advanced technology of aeroponics, you'll be able to enjoy fresh, healthy herbs year-round. These methods not only maximize space but also ensure that your plants receive optimal care, resulting in bountiful harvests that enhance your culinary and medicinal pursuits.

10.4 MAXIMIZING LIGHT AND SPACE FOR INDOOR GARDENS

Light is a critical factor in the growth and health of your indoor herbs. Without sufficient light, herbs can become leggy and weak, struggling to produce the vibrant flavors and potent medicinal properties they are known for. Understanding light intensity and duration is key. Most herbs require at least six hours of direct sunlight each day. If your indoor space lacks this, consider placing your herbs in south-facing windows, which typically receive the most consistent light throughout the day. The intensity of light diminishes with distance, so keeping your herbs as close to the light source as possible will ensure they receive the energy needed for robust growth.

Optimizing natural light in your indoor space can significantly enhance your herb garden's productivity. Reflective surfaces, such as mirrors or white walls, can help increase light exposure by bouncing light around the room. Position these surfaces strategically to maximize the amount of light reaching your plants. Regularly rotating your pots is another effective strategy. This ensures that all sides of the plant receive equal light, preventing uneven growth and promoting a well-rounded, healthy plant. Additionally, removing any obstructions that block light from reaching your herbs is crucial. Trim back any overhanging foliage or relocate objects that cast shadows, ensuring your herbs bask in unobstructed sunlight.

When natural light is insufficient, artificial lighting solutions can bridge the gap. LED grow lights are a popular choice for indoor gardening due to their energy efficiency and customizable light spectrums. These lights can be adjusted to provide the specific wavelengths of light that plants need for photosynthesis, making them highly effective for herb growth. Fluorescent lights, particularly T5 and T8 models, are another affordable and widely available option. They provide a broad spectrum of light and are suitable for small spaces. Compact fluorescent lights (CFLs) are ideal for those with limited space, as they can be fitted into standard light fixtures. High-intensity discharge (HID) lights are powerful and provide intense light, but they require more energy and can generate significant heat, necessitating good ventilation.

Maximizing limited indoor space requires creative solutions. Stacking shelves with grow lights allows you to create vertical gardens, making efficient use of vertical space. Each shelf can house different herbs, ensuring they receive adequate light from the grow lights installed above. Tiered plant stands are another excellent option, providing multiple levels for your herbs and enhancing the aesthetic appeal of your indoor garden. Hanging planters from the ceiling can save valuable floor space while adding a dynamic element to your garden. These planters are perfect for trailing herbs like mint or oregano. Utilizing windowsills and countertops efficiently can also make a significant difference. Place herbs in these spaces to take advantage of natural light, and use compact, stackable containers to maximize the area.

Incorporating these strategies into your indoor herb gardening routine will ensure that your plants receive the light they need to thrive, regardless of the limitations of your indoor space. By understanding the importance of light intensity and duration, optimizing natural light, utilizing artificial lighting solutions, and employing space-saving techniques, you can create a flourishing indoor herb garden that provides fresh, flavorful, and medicinally potent herbs year-round.

Light and space are crucial elements in successful indoor herb gardening. By maximizing both, you can ensure your herbs thrive and provide you with a continuous supply of fresh, flavorful, and medicinally beneficial plants. In the next chapter, we will explore advanced techniques and troubleshooting tips to further enhance your herb gardening skills.

CHAPTER 11
ADVANCED TECHNIQUES
AND TROUBLESHOOTING

The process of turning a single plant into many has always fascinated me, and it's one of the most rewarding aspects of herb gardening. In this chapter, we'll delve into the advanced techniques of propagating herbs from cuttings and seeds, providing you with the knowledge to expand your garden efficiently and cost-effectively.

11.1 PROPAGATING HERBS FROM CUTTINGS AND SEEDS

Propagation is a fantastic way to expand your herb garden without continually purchasing new plants. One of the significant benefits is cost-effectiveness. Instead of buying multiple plants, you can grow many from just one. This method ensures genetic consistency, which means the new plants will have the same characteristics as the parent plant. This is particularly important if you have a plant with exceptional flavor, disease resistance, or other desirable traits. Another advantage is the preservation of heirloom varieties. By propagating these plants, you maintain their unique genetic makeup, contributing to biodiversity and the continuation of heritage plants.

To begin propagating herbs from cuttings, start by selecting healthy parent plants. Choose plants that are vigorous, disease-free, and have strong, healthy growth. Using clean, sharp scissors or pruning shears, cut a 4-6 inch section from the tip of a stem. Remove the lower leaves, leaving a few at the top. This helps the cutting focus its energy on root development rather than maintaining foliage. Place the cuttings in water or a rooting medium, such as a mix of perlite and peat. Maintaining humidity is crucial, so cover the cuttings with a plastic bag or place them in a propagator. Ensure they receive bright, indirect light. Direct sunlight can be too intense and dry out the cuttings before they root.

Certain herbs respond exceptionally well to propagation from cuttings. Mint is incredibly fast-growing and easy to root, making it an excellent choice for beginners. Simply place mint cuttings in water, and within a few days, roots will start to form. Basil is another herb that propagates quickly. You can see roots developing in water in just a few days, and once established, the new plants can be transplanted into soil. Rosemary requires a bit more patience but is highly rewarding. It's best to use a rooting hormone to encourage root growth and keep the cuttings in a warm, humid environment.

Starting herbs from seeds is another effective method, offering its own set of benefits. Seeds allow for a wider variety of herbs, including rare and heirloom varieties that might not be available as plants. For some herbs, advanced techniques like stratification and scarification can improve germination rates. Stratification involves pre-treating seeds that require a period of cold to germinate. Place the seeds in a damp paper towel, seal them in a plastic bag, and refrigerate for a few weeks. This mimics the natural winter conditions the seeds would experience in the wild. Scarification involves abrading the seed coat to promote germination. This can be done by gently rubbing the seeds with sandpaper or nicking them with a knife.

Using seedling heat mats can provide consistent warmth, which is essential for germinating many herb seeds. Place the seed trays on the heat mats and maintain a steady temperature around 70-75°F. This warmth encourages quicker and more uniform germination. Once the seedlings have developed a few sets of true leaves, they can be transplanted into larger pots or directly into the garden. When transplanting, handle the seedlings gently by the leaves, not the stems, to avoid damaging the delicate plants. Ensure the soil is well-prepared and enriched with compost to give the young plants the best start.

Propagation, whether from cuttings or seeds, is a skill that enhances your gardening experience. It allows you to multiply your favorite herbs, preserve heirloom varieties, and experiment with new plants. By understanding and mastering these techniques, you can create a diverse, thriving herb garden that provides culinary and medicinal benefits year-round.

11.2 TROUBLESHOOTING COMMON GROWTH ISSUES

Herb gardening can sometimes be a puzzle, with plants showing signs of distress despite your best efforts. One of the most common issues you might encounter is yellowing leaves. This often signals nutrient deficiencies or overwatering. When older leaves turn yellow first, it usually points to a nitrogen deficiency. Nitrogen is vital for leafy growth, and without it, plants can't produce the chlorophyll needed to keep their leaves green. To correct this, use a nitrogen-rich fertilizer like fish emulsion or compost tea. If the yellowing is more general and affects newer leaves, it might be due to overwatering. Overwatered plants often have soggy soil and poor root health. Ensure your pots have proper drainage and let the soil dry out slightly between waterings.

Wilting plants can be another distressing sight. This can indicate either underwatering or root rot. If your plant's soil is dry, under-watering is the likely culprit. Water thoroughly, ensuring moisture reaches deep into the soil. Conversely, if the soil is wet and the plant still wilts, suspect root rot. Root rot is caused by fungal infections in waterlogged soil. To address this, improve drainage and consider repotting the plant in fresh soil. Cutting back on watering frequency until the plant recovers can also help.

Stunted growth is another common problem. Poor soil quality or inadequate light usually causes this. Herbs need nutrient-rich soil with good drainage. If your soil is compacted or lacks organic matter, it can stunt growth. Amend the soil with compost or well-rotted manure to improve its structure and fertility. Inadequate light can also lead to stunted growth. Herbs generally need at least six hours of direct sunlight daily. If your plants are leggy and pale, they likely need more light. Move them to a sunnier spot or supplement with grow lights.

Leaf spots and discoloration often point to disease or pest infestations. Fungal diseases can cause brown or black spots on leaves, often spreading in humid conditions. Ensure good air circulation around your plants and avoid overhead watering to keep the foliage dry. If you spot these symptoms, remove affected leaves and treat the plant with an organic fungicide like neem oil. Pest infestations, such as aphids or spider mites, can also cause discoloration. Inspect your plants regularly and use insecticidal soap or neem oil to control pests.

Nitrogen deficiency, identified by yellowing older leaves, can be addressed with nitrogen-rich fertilizers. Phosphorus deficiency, which gives leaves a purplish tint, can be corrected with bone meal or rock phosphate. Potassium deficiency, marked by browning leaf edges, can be remedied with potassium-rich fertilizers like kelp meal or wood ash. Regularly testing your soil can help you catch these deficiencies early and take corrective action.

Overwatering and underwatering both present unique challenges. Overwatered plants often have yellow leaves and mushy roots. Ensure your pots have drainage holes and use a well-draining soil mix. Allow the soil to dry out before watering again. Underwatered plants, on the other hand, have dry, brittle leaves and soil that pulls away from the pot's edges. Water thoroughly, ensuring the water reaches the plant's roots. Using mulch can help retain soil moisture and reduce the frequency of watering needed.

Light conditions are crucial for healthy herb growth. Signs of insufficient light include slow growth, pale leaves, and plants leaning toward the light source. To improve light conditions, place your herbs in a south-facing window where they receive ample sunlight. If natural light is limited, consider using LED grow lights. These provide the full spectrum of light needed for photosynthesis and can be adjusted to ensure your herbs get enough light.

Regularly rotating your pots can also help your plants receive even light exposure. This prevents them from becoming leggy and ensures balanced growth. Using reflective surfaces like mirrors or white walls can increase the amount of light your plants receive. These simple adjustments can make a significant difference in your herbs' health and productivity.

Understanding these common growth issues and their solutions will empower you to maintain a thriving herb garden. Identifying symptoms early and taking corrective action can prevent minor problems from becoming major setbacks. With careful attention to watering, soil quality, and light conditions, your herb garden can flourish, providing you with an abundant supply of fresh, flavorful, and health beneficial herbs.

11.3 ENHANCING SOIL FERTILITY WITH COMPOSTING

Creating and maintaining a compost pile is one of the most rewarding activities you can undertake as a gardener. Composting significantly enhances soil health, leading to a more fertile and productive garden. When you add compost to your soil, it improves the structure, making it looser and better able to retain water. This is particularly important for herbs, which thrive in well-draining yet moisture-retentive soil. Compost also provides essential nutrients that plants need for growth. Unlike synthetic fertilizers, compost releases nutrients slowly, ensuring a steady supply over time. Additionally, compost supports beneficial microbial activity, which is crucial for breaking down organic matter and making nutrients available to plants.

Starting a compost pile is relatively straightforward but requires some planning. First, choose a location for your compost pile or bin. Ideally, it should be in a shaded area that is easily accessible yet out of direct sight. This placement helps maintain moisture levels and keeps the compost from drying out too quickly. Next, balance green (nitrogen-rich) and brown (carbon-rich) materials. Green materials include kitchen scraps, grass clippings, and coffee grounds, while brown materials consist of leaves, straw, and cardboard. A good rule of thumb is to use roughly equal parts of green and brown materials. Turning the compost regularly is vital for aeration and speeding up decomposition. Use a pitchfork or compost aerator to mix the pile every few weeks. Monitor moisture levels; the compost should be as damp as a wrung-out sponge. If it's too dry, add water; if it's too wet, add more brown materials to absorb excess moisture.

Different types of composting systems can suit various needs and spaces. The traditional compost pile is simple and effective for larger gardens. It involves piling organic materials in a designated area and turning them regularly.

Compost Bins

Compost bins are more contained and tidier, making them ideal for urban settings. These bins can be purchased or homemade and help keep the composting process neat and contained.

Vermicomposting

Vermicomposting uses worms to break down organic matter. This method is excellent for small spaces and can even be done indoors. Worm bins require a balance of green and brown materials and should be kept moist but not waterlogged.

Bokashi Composting

Bokashi composting is a fermentation method for kitchen scraps. It involves adding scraps to a bin with a special bran that contains beneficial microbes. The scraps ferment over a few weeks and then can be buried in the garden to decompose further.

Using finished compost in your garden can significantly enhance soil fertility. One effective method is top-dressing plants with a layer of compost. Spread a thin layer around the base of your herbs, being careful not to cover the stems. This method provides a slow-release fertilizer and helps retain soil moisture. Mixing compost into garden beds before planting is another great way to enrich the soil. Work the compost into the top few inches of soil to ensure it's well-integrated. Compost tea is a liquid extract of compost that can be used for foliar feeding. To make compost tea, fill a burlap sack or other porous bag with compost and steep it in water for a few days. Use the resulting liquid to spray your plants, providing them with a quick nutrient boost.

Composting not only reduces waste but also closes the nutrient loop, returning valuable organic matter to the soil. The process is a fundamental aspect of sustainable gardening, ensuring that your herbs have the best possible growing conditions. By incorporating compost into your gardening routine, you create a fertile, healthy environment that supports robust plant growth and enhances the flavor and medicinal properties of your herbs.

11.4 INTEGRATING PERMACULTURE PRINCIPLES

Permaculture is a gardening philosophy that emphasizes creating sustainable and self-sufficient ecosystems. The goal is to design gardens that work in harmony with nature, rather than against it. This approach not only benefits the garden but also promotes environmental stewardship. By mimicking natural processes, permaculture gardens become more resilient and require fewer external inputs. This means less labor for you and a healthier environment for your plants. The principles of permaculture can be applied to herb gardening, making it possible to cultivate a thriving, sustainable herb garden that supports both your needs and the ecosystem.

One of the core principles of permaculture is to observe and interact with your garden environment. Spend time understanding how sunlight moves across your space, where water collects, and what types of plants naturally thrive there. This observation helps you make informed decisions about plant placement and garden design. For instance, if you notice that a particular area receives more sunlight, it might be the perfect spot for sun-loving herbs like basil and rosemary. On the other hand, shaded areas could support mint and parsley. By observing and interacting with your garden, you create a space that's tailored to the natural conditions of your environment.

Another vital principle is to catch and store energy. This involves utilizing natural resources efficiently to ensure your garden is productive year-round. For example, rainwater harvesting is a practical way to catch and store water. Install rain barrels to collect runoff from your roof and use this stored water to irrigate your herbs during dry spells. Solar energy can also be harnessed by placing reflective materials around your garden to increase light exposure. These practices not only conserve resources but also reduce your garden's dependency on external inputs, making it more self-sufficient.

Obtaining a yield is about ensuring your garden is productive and resilient. This principle emphasizes the importance of creating a garden that provides a continuous supply of herbs, whether for culinary or holistic health purposes. Companion planting is a technique that supports this principle. By planting herbs that support each other, you can enhance growth and deter pests. For example, planting basil near tomatoes can improve the flavor of the tomatoes and repel harmful insects. Similarly, growing chives alongside carrots can help deter carrot flies. This approach maximizes the productivity of your garden while minimizing the need for chemical interventions.

Applying self-regulation and accepting feedback is essential for long-term success. This principle encourages you to learn from your gardening experiences and adapt your practices accordingly. Keep a gardening journal to track what works and what doesn't. If you notice that a particular herb isn't thriving, take the time to understand why and make adjustments. Maybe it needs more sunlight or better soil drainage. By being responsive to the feedback your garden provides, you can continuously improve and create a more resilient and productive space.

Permaculture also involves practical techniques that can be easily integrated into your herb garden. Mulching is one such technique that conserves moisture and improves soil health. Apply a layer of organic mulch, such as straw or wood chips, around your herbs. This helps retain soil moisture, suppress weeds, and gradually adds organic matter to the soil as it decomposes. Another technique is creating microclimates by using structures and plants to modify environmental conditions. For instance, planting taller herbs or erecting trellises can provide shade and wind protection for more delicate plants. This creates a more favorable growing environment for all your herbs.

Water harvesting is another practical permaculture technique. Beyond rain barrels, you can design your garden to capture and direct water flow. Swales, which are shallow trenches dug along the contour of the land, can capture runoff and direct it to areas that need more moisture. This not only conserves water but also reduces erosion and improves soil health. By integrating these techniques, you create a garden that is not only productive but also environmentally sustainable.

The benefits of adopting a permaculture approach are numerous. Enhanced biodiversity and ecosystem health are among the most significant advantages. By creating a garden that mimics natural ecosystems, you support a wide range of beneficial insects, birds, and other wildlife. This biodiversity helps control pests naturally and improves pollination, leading to healthier and more productive plants. Additionally, permaculture practices reduce the need for external inputs like chemical fertilizers and pesticides, making your garden more sustainable and cost-effective.

Another significant benefit is increased resilience to environmental stressors. A permaculture garden is designed to withstand extreme weather conditions, pests, and diseases. For instance, by planting a diverse range of herbs, you ensure that even if one species is affected by a pest or disease, others will continue to thrive. This diversity also improves soil health, making it more resistant to erosion and nutrient depletion. Improved soil fertility and plant health are direct results of these practices, leading to a more robust and productive garden.

By incorporating permaculture principles into your herb gardening, you create a sustainable, self-sufficient ecosystem that supports your needs and those of the environment. This approach not only enhances the productivity of your garden but also contributes to the health and resilience of the broader ecosystem. Embrace these principles, and you'll find that your garden becomes a thriving, dynamic space that provides an abundance of herbs for culinary and holistic health uses.

CHAPTER 12
PLANNING AND MAINTAINING YOUR HERB GARDEN

T his chapter is dedicated to helping you create a comprehensive, year-round gardening plan, ensuring that your herb garden thrives in every season.

12.1 CREATING A YEAR-ROUND GARDENING PLAN

Planning ahead is crucial for maintaining a productive herb garden throughout the year. By establishing a year-round gardening plan, you can ensure continuous productivity and minimize downtime. Regular planting and harvesting schedules allow you to make the most of each season, while staggering planting times provides a continuous yield of fresh herbs. Planning for seasonal transitions, such as preparing for winter or gearing up for spring planting, ensures that your garden remains active and productive.

A well-structured gardening calendar is an invaluable tool for mapping out your activities. Start by listing monthly planting and harvesting tasks. For instance, in early spring, focus on starting seeds indoors for herbs like basil and parsley. As the weather warms, transplant these seedlings into the garden. Summer months may involve regular harvesting and maintenance, while fall tasks could include harvesting late-season herbs and preparing the garden for winter. Seasonal maintenance activities, such as mulching in the fall or pruning in the early spring, should also be incorporated into your plan.

Important dates for starting seeds indoors or transplanting are critical to your success. Use tools like the USDA Plant Hardiness Zone maps to determine your local frost dates and growing seasons. For example, if you live in a region with a last frost date in early May, plan to start seeds indoors six to eight weeks prior. This ensures that your seedlings are ready for transplanting once the danger of frost has passed. Similarly, knowing your first frost date in the fall allows you to plan your final harvest and prepare your garden for winter.

Climate plays a significant role in your gardening plan. Adjust your schedule based on local climate conditions to ensure the best results. For colder climates, focus on cold-hardy herbs like chives and mint, which can withstand frost. Plan to start these seeds indoors and transplant them once the weather warms. In hotter climates, consider herbs like rosemary and thyme, which thrive in dry conditions. Adjust your watering schedule to accommodate the increased heat and consider using shade cloths to protect delicate herbs from intense sunlight.

Weather-related challenges, such as unexpected frosts or heatwaves, can disrupt your gardening plan. Stay informed about local weather forecasts and be prepared to adjust your activities accordingly. For example, if a late frost is predicted, cover your seedlings with frost blankets to protect them. During heatwaves, increase your watering frequency and consider providing temporary shade for your herbs. Selecting climate-appropriate herbs, such as drought-tolerant varieties for arid regions or moisture-loving herbs for humid climates, ensures that your garden remains resilient in the face of changing conditions.

To maximize garden productivity throughout the year, employ strategies like succession planting, cover cropping, and using cold frames and greenhouses. Succession planting involves sowing seeds at regular intervals to ensure a continuous harvest. For example, plant a new batch of basil every two to three weeks during the growing season. This staggered approach ensures that you always have fresh herbs available.

Cover cropping is an excellent way to improve soil health during the off-season. Planting cover crops like clover or rye in late fall enriches the soil with organic matter and nutrients as they decompose. These crops also help prevent soil erosion and suppress weeds, providing a head start for your spring planting. Using cold frames and greenhouses extends your growing season by creating a microclimate that protects your herbs from frost and extreme weather. Cold frames are simple structures with transparent covers that trap heat and protect plants, while greenhouses offer more comprehensive environmental control.

Incorporating these strategies into your year-round gardening plan ensures that your herb garden remains productive and thriving throughout the year. By planning ahead, adjusting for climate conditions, and employing techniques like succession planting and cover cropping, you can enjoy a continuous supply of fresh, flavorful, and medicinally beneficial herbs.

12.2 RECORD KEEPING AND GARDEN JOURNALING

Keeping detailed garden records is more than just a chore; it's an invaluable tool that helps you monitor plant growth and health, identify successful and unsuccessful practices, and track weather patterns and their impact on your garden. By documenting your observations, you create a treasure trove of information to refer to, making each gardening season more successful than the last. Imagine the satisfaction of knowing exactly when your basil thrives best, or which organic pest control method worked wonders on your mint. Detailed records transform your gardening efforts from guesswork into a well-informed practice.

Setting up a garden journal doesn't have to be complicated. Start with sections for planting dates, harvest quantities, and pest issues. These basic categories will help you keep track of when you planted each herb, how much you harvested, and any pest problems you encountered. Add space for notes on observations and experiments. Did you try a new watering technique? How did it affect your plants? Documenting these details helps you learn and improve. Including photos for visual reference can be incredibly helpful. A picture of your thriving rosemary in June compared to its state in September can reveal a lot about how well it adapted to seasonal changes. Templates for weekly and monthly updates keep your record-keeping consistent and manageable.

For tech-savvy gardeners, digital tools and apps offer a modern solution for record keeping. Garden planning apps like Seedtime allow you to visualize when to seed, transplant, or harvest crops based on your local area. Digital journals and spreadsheets offer the flexibility to tag entries, link to specific plantings, and add pictures, making it easy to track your garden's progress. Online gardening communities provide a platform to share your records and gain insights from fellow gardeners. These tools not only streamline the process but also enhance your ability to analyze and utilize your records effectively.

Analyzing your garden records is where the real magic happens. At the end of each season, take the time to review your entries. Identify patterns and trends that emerge. Did certain herbs consistently perform well in a particular spot? Did others struggle with pests more than usual? Use these insights to adjust your plans for the following year. If you notice that your basil thrived when planted in partial shade rather than full sun, you can replicate that success next season. If a particular organic fertilizer resulted in lush, healthy growth, make it a staple in your gardening routine. By continuously refining your approach based on past experiences, you create a cycle of improvement that leads to a more productive and rewarding herb garden.

Visual Element: Garden Journal Layout Example

- **Planting Dates**: Record the exact date you planted each herb.
- **Harvest Quantities**: Note the amount harvested and the date.
- **Pest Issues**: Document any pest problems and solutions tried.
- **Observations and Experiments**: Record the results of new techniques or changes.
- **Photos**: Include pictures of your garden at different stages.
- **Weekly and Monthly Updates**: Use templates to ensure consistency.

Keeping detailed garden records might seem like extra work, but the benefits far outweigh the effort. By monitoring plant growth and health, identifying successful practices, and tracking weather patterns, you create a comprehensive guide that helps you improve your gardening efforts season after season. Whether you prefer a traditional journal or a digital tool, the key is to be consistent and thorough. In doing so, you set yourself up for a thriving herb garden that not only meets but exceeds your expectations.

12.3 SUSTAINABLE PRACTICES FOR LONG-TERM SUCCESS

Sustainable gardening is more than just a buzzword; it's a commitment to practices that protect the environment and promote long-term garden health. One of the key principles is reducing reliance on synthetic inputs. Synthetic fertilizers and pesticides may offer quick fixes, but they can harm the soil and local ecosystem over time. Natural alternatives and organic methods, such as composting and using beneficial insects for pest control, offer sustainable solutions that enrich the soil and maintain ecological balance. Another vital aspect of sustainability is conserving water and soil resources. Water is a precious resource, and efficient use ensures that your garden thrives without waste. Soil conservation involves practices that prevent erosion and maintain fertility, ensuring that the land remains productive year after year.

Water conservation is a cornerstone of sustainable gardening. One effective strategy is installing rain barrels to collect rainwater. This not only reduces your dependence on municipal water supplies but also provides your plants with naturally soft water, free of chemicals. Using drip irrigation systems is another excellent method. Drip irrigation delivers water directly to the plant roots, minimizing evaporation and runoff. This targeted approach ensures that your herbs receive the moisture they need without wasting water. Mulching is also incredibly beneficial for water conservation. By covering the soil with organic materials like straw or wood chips, you can significantly reduce evaporation, retain soil moisture, and even suppress weeds. This simple practice can make a big difference in maintaining soil health and conserving water.

Crop rotation and polyculture are powerful techniques for improving soil health and reducing pest and disease pressures. Rotating herbs with different nutrient needs prevents the depletion of specific nutrients and breaks the cycle of pests and diseases that target particular plants. For example, following nitrogen-hungry basil with nitrogen-fixing legumes can naturally replenish soil fertility. Polyculture, or planting diverse species together, creates a balanced ecosystem that supports beneficial insects and discourages pests. Avoiding monocultures, where a single crop is grown in large quantities, reduces the risk of pest and disease buildup. By diversifying your garden with a variety of herbs and companion plants, you create a resilient environment that can withstand challenges more effectively.

Building and maintaining healthy soil is the foundation of a successful garden. Regularly adding organic matter, such as compost or well-rotted manure, enriches the soil with essential nutrients and improves its structure. This practice enhances water retention and aeration, creating an ideal environment for root growth. Using green manures and cover crops, like clover or rye, adds organic matter and nutrients to the soil when turned under. These crops also help prevent erosion and improve soil structure. Avoiding soil compaction is equally important. Compacted soil restricts root growth and reduces aeration, making it difficult for plants to access water and nutrients. To prevent this, avoid walking on garden beds and use raised beds or designated paths. Mulching also helps protect the soil surface from erosion and compaction, ensuring that it remains fertile and productive.

Sustainable gardening is a holistic approach that considers the long-term health of the garden and the environment. By reducing reliance on synthetic inputs, conserving water and soil resources, enhancing biodiversity, and employing practices like crop rotation and polyculture, you create a thriving, resilient garden. These practices not only benefit your herbs but also contribute to the health of the broader ecosystem.

12.4 COMMUNITY GARDENING AND SHARING YOUR HARVEST

Participating in community gardens offers numerous benefits that go beyond just growing herbs. Engaging with experienced gardeners allows you to learn from their tried-and-true methods and avoid common pitfalls. The shared resources and tools available in community gardens mean you don't have to invest heavily in all the equipment yourself. Plus, the sense of community fostered by these gardens can be immensely rewarding. You become part of a group that shares your passion for gardening, creating bonds over shared successes and challenges. This collective effort not only makes gardening more enjoyable but also more productive.

Finding and joining local gardening groups can be a straightforward process. Start by searching online for community gardens in your area. Websites dedicated to local events or community boards often list gardening groups and their meeting times. Attending workshops and events related to gardening is another excellent way to get involved. These events are not only educational but also provide opportunities to meet like-minded individuals who can guide you on your gardening journey. Volunteering at community garden projects is another fantastic way to immerse yourself in the gardening community. By offering your time and effort, you gain hands-on experience and build relationships with other gardeners.

Sharing your harvest is a practice that benefits both you and your community. When you have an abundance of herbs, sharing them reduces food waste and ensures that nothing goes to waste. Local food banks and shelters greatly appreciate fresh produce, and your contributions can make a significant difference. Sharing your harvest also builds goodwill and fosters a sense of community spirit. Imagine the joy of giving a neighbor a bundle of fresh basil or the satisfaction of knowing your excess mint is being used in a local soup kitchen. These small acts of kindness contribute to a stronger, more connected community.

Organizing garden swaps and events is a wonderful way to share your knowledge and harvest with others. Hosting a seed and plant swap allows gardeners to exchange seeds and plants, diversifying their gardens and trying new varieties without spending extra money. Community potlucks featuring homegrown herbs are another great idea. These events bring people together to share meals made with fresh, local ingredients, and they provide an opportunity to showcase the culinary uses of your herbs. Gardening workshops and demonstrations are excellent for sharing your expertise with others. By teaching what you've learned, you help others succeed in their gardening endeavors and contribute to the collective knowledge of your community.

Interactive Element: How to Host a Seed Swap

- Choose a Location: Find a community center, park, or even a large backyard.
- Invite Participants: Reach out to local gardening groups, friends, and neighbors.
- Set Guidelines: Ensure participants label their seeds clearly and provide basic growing information.
- Provide Supplies: Have envelopes, markers, and tables available for organizing seeds.
- Facilitate Exchanges: Encourage participants to share stories and tips about their seeds and plants.

Community gardening and sharing your harvest bring numerous benefits, from enhancing your skills and building connections to reducing waste and supporting local causes. These practices not only enrich your gardening experience but also contribute to a more sustainable and connected community. As we wrap up this chapter, remember that gardening is not just a solitary activity but a communal one that can bring people together and create lasting bonds. By actively participating in community gardens and sharing your bounty, you become part of something larger, contributing to a healthier, more resilient community.

CONCLUSION

As we reach the end of our journey together, it's important to take a moment to reflect on all that we've explored and learned throughout this book. From the initial excitement of starting your organic herb garden to understanding the nuances of soil health, watering techniques, and pest management, you have gained a wealth of knowledge that can transform any patch of soil or windowsill into a thriving herb haven.

We began with the foundational principles of organic herb gardening. You learned that organic gardening isn't just about avoiding synthetic chemicals. It's about creating a harmonious ecosystem where plants, soil, and beneficial insects work together. We delved into the importance of soil health, composting, and the use of natural fertilizers. Remember, healthy soil is the cornerstone of any successful garden. By feeding your soil with organic matter, you support the microorganisms that keep your garden vibrant and productive.

You discovered the joy of selecting the right herbs for your garden. Whether it's basil for your summer pesto, mint for refreshing iced teas, or lavender to soothe your senses, choosing the right herbs is the first step to a fulfilling gardening experience. We covered the specific needs of various herbs, from their preferred growing conditions to their culinary and holistic health uses.

Setting up your gardening space, whether on a windowsill, balcony, or backyard, was another key topic. You learned about the importance of sunlight, air circulation, and proper plant spacing. You now know how to create a garden layout that maximizes space and ensures each plant gets what it needs to thrive.

Watering techniques and soil health management were crucial aspects we discussed. You now understand the specific watering needs of different herbs and the impact of climate on their hydration. Efficient watering methods like drip irrigation and mulching help conserve water and maintain soil moisture. These practices are essential for keeping your herbs healthy and productive.

We explored the challenges of growing herbs in various climates, from hot and dry regions to cold and frosty areas and provided strategies to overcome these challenges. You learned about drought-tolerant herbs, frost protection techniques, and the importance of soil management in humid and tropical climates.

Harvesting and preserving herbs were also covered extensively. You now know when your herbs are at their peak for harvesting and the best methods for drying, freezing, and making infusions and tinctures. These skills ensure that you can enjoy the benefits of your herbs long after they've been harvested.

We also delved into the culinary and holistic health uses of herbs, providing you with recipes and tips on how to make the most of your garden's bounty. From delicious herb-infused oils to soothing teas and effective salves, you now have the tools to enhance your culinary creations and support your health naturally.

Finally, we addressed the advanced techniques of propagation, troubleshooting common growth issues, and integrating sustainable practices. You learned how to propagate herbs from cuttings and seeds, diagnose and solve problems like nutrient deficiencies and pest infestations, and embrace sustainable gardening practices that support long-term garden health.

Now, armed with this knowledge, it's time to act. Start by choosing a few herbs you love and begin your garden, whether it's a small windowsill planter or a full backyard plot. Pay attention to your soil, water wisely, and monitor your plants for any signs of stress. Keep a garden journal to track your progress and learn from your experiences. Don't be afraid to experiment and try new techniques. Gardening is a journey of continuous learning and discovery.

Thank you for joining me on this journey. Your dedication and enthusiasm for herb gardening is truly inspiring. I hope this book has provided you with the knowledge and confidence to cultivate your own herb garden. Remember, the rewards of herb gardening go beyond the fresh flavors and health benefits. It's about connecting with nature, experiencing the joy of nurturing plants, and creating a sustainable environment.

Embrace the joys and challenges of gardening with an open heart and a curious mind. Every plant you grow, every leaf you harvest, and every tea you brew is a testament to your dedication and love for nature. Your garden reflects you, and I am honored to have been a part of your gardening journey.

Happy gardening! May your herb garden thrive and bring you endless joy and fulfillment.

Warm regards, The Grinning Gardener

REFERENCES

- Garden Organic. (n.d.). *Principles of organic gardening.* Garden Organic. https://www.gardenorganic.org.uk/expert-advice/principles-of-organic-gardening
- Better Homes & Gardens. (n.d.). *15 of the easiest herbs to grow for beginners.* https://www.bhg.com/gardening/vegetable/herbs/easy-to-grow-herbs/
- Real Simple. (n.d.). *How to grow an indoor herb garden.* https://www.realsimple.com/how-to-grow-an-indoor-herb-garden-7376389
- Garden Design. (n.d.). *12 essential garden tools for the beginner.* https://www.gardendesign.com/how-to/tools.html
- Oregon State University Extension Service. (n.d.). *How do I test my garden soil* Oregon State University. https://extension.oregonstate.edu/gardening/soil-compost/how-do-i-test-my-garden-soil
- Oregon State University Extension Service. (n.d.). *Improving garden soils with organic matter* (EC 1561). Oregon State University. https://extension.oregonstate.edu/catalog/pub/ec-1561-improving-garden-soils-organic-matter
- Celebrated Herb. (n.d.). *What you need to know about fertilizing herbs: Nurturing your plants.* https://celebratedherb.com/what-you-need-to-know-about-fertilizing-herbs/
- Grow Sow Happy. (n.d.). *Direct seed vs transplant: Choosing the best planting method.* https://www.growsowhappy.com/blog/direct-seed-or-transplant#:
- Swan Hose. (n.d.). *A guide to watering herbs—Best practices for a healthy herb garden.* https://swanhose.com/blogs/watering-herbs/a-guide-to-watering-herbs-best-practices-for-a-healthy-herb-gardensrsltid=AfmBOoqb3QuVmZi_4Hzu4Dw9mNCpe-BqFyUsYr52z3CnaFdXTiVWNl4gP

- Odyssey Group. (n.d.). *The benefits of mulching for soil health and plant growth.* https://odysseygroupllc.com/landscape/benefits-of-mulching-soil-health-plant-growth/
- Horiba. (n.d.). *Soil pH and nutrient availability.* https://www.horiba.com/usa/water-quality/applications/agriculture-crop-science/soil-ph-and-nutrient-availability/
- Epic Gardening. (n.d.). *21 heat-tolerant herbs for hot climates.* https://www.epicgardening.com/heat-tolerant-herbs/
- NC State Extension. (n.d.). *Winterizing the herb garden.* https://content.ces.ncsu.edu/winterizing-the-herb-garden
- Helpful Gardener. (n.d.). *Herbs that grow well in tropical heat.* https://www.helpfulgardener.com/forum/viewtopic.phpt=56851
- Mahoney's Garden Center. (n.d.). *Salt-tolerant plants for a thriving coastal garden.* https://mahoneysgarden.com/salt-tolerant-plants-falmouth/
- Master Gardeners of Northern Virginia. (n.d.). *Season-by-season guide to growing herbs.* https://mgnv.org/plants/veg-herbs/seasonal-guide-growing-herbs/
- Bonnie Plants. (n.d.). *Harvesting your summer herb garden.* https://bonnieplants.com/blogs/garden-fundamentals/summer-herb-harvest-tips
- NC State Extension. (n.d.). *Harvesting and preserving herbs for the home gardener.* https://content.ces.ncsu.edu/harvesting-and-preserving-herbs-for-the-home-gardener
- Fine Gardening. (n.d.). *How to grow herbs indoors in winter.* https://www.finegardening.com/project-guides/fruits-and-vegetables/grow-herbs-indoors-this-winter
- Gardening Know How. (n.d.). *Herb growing problems: Common herb garden pests and solutions.* https://www.gardeningknowhow.com/edible/herbs/hgen/herb-growing-problems.htm
- NC State Extension. (n.d.). *Integrated pest management (IPM).* https://content.ces.ncsu.edu/extension-gardener-handbook/8-integrated-pest-management-ipm
- Mount Sinai. (n.d.). *Herbal medicine information.* https://www.mountsinai.org/health-library/treatment/herbal-medicine
- Monrovia. (n.d.). *Beneficial insects for a healthy garden: A visual guide.* https://www.monrovia.com/be-

inspired/beneficial-insects-for-a-healthy-
garden.htmlsrsltid=AfmBOop-gCCP58DTu2F6U5ZMup-
DsjqBn3v9qdPxICc_92L6qirmgE186

- NC State Extension. (n.d.). *Harvesting and preserving herbs
for the home gardener.* https://content.ces.ncsu.edu/
harvesting-and-preserving-herbs-for-the-home-
gardener#:.

- The Spruce Eats. (n.d.). *4 simple ways to dry herbs.* https://
www.thespruceeats.com/harvesting-and-drying-leafy-
herbs-1327541

- Serious Eats. (n.d.). *Freeze fresh herbs for long-term storage.*
https://www.seriouseats.com/how-to-freeze-herbs-for-
long-term-storage

- The Spruce Eats. (n.d.). *How to make herbal infusions.*
https://www.thespruceeats.com/how-to-make-an-herbal-
infusion-1762142

- MasterClass. (n.d.). *Cooking 101: The 15 most common
culinary herbs and how to cook with them.* https://www.
masterclass.com/articles/cooking-101-the-15-most-
common-culinary-herbs-and-how-to-cook-with-them

- Sustained Kitchen. (2020, March 4). *Ultimate guide to herbs.*
https://www.sustained.kitchen/latest/2020/3/4/guide-to-
herbs

- Bon Appétit. (n.d.). *How to use up all of those %@! fresh herbs.*
https://www.bonappetit.com/test-kitchen/ingredients/
article/what-to-do-with-herbs

- Black Gold. (n.d.). *How to make herb-infused vinegars and oils.*
https://blackgold.bz/how-to-make-herb-infused-
vinegars-and-oils/

- Srivastava, J. K., Shankar, E., & Gupta, S. (2010).
Chamomile: A herbal medicine of the past with bright future.
National Institutes of Health. https://www.ncbi.nlm.nih.
gov/pmc/articles/PMC2995283/

- Sharma, M., & Anderson, S. A. (2014). *Echinacea—A source
of potent antivirals for respiratory infections.* National
Institutes of Health. https://www.ncbi.nlm.nih.gov/pmc/
articles/PMC4058675/

- Lovely Greens. (n.d.). *How to make lavender oil: A step-by-
step guide.* https://lovelygreens.com/how-to-make-
lavender-oil/

- Healthline. (n.d.). *12 science-backed benefits of peppermint tea and extracts*. https://www.healthline.com/nutrition/peppermint-tea
- Herbs at Home. (n.d.). *How to pick the best pot for growing herbs*. https://herbsathome.co/best-pot-for-herbs/#:
- Martha Stewart. (n.d.). *How to build an herb spiral—a compact raised garden bed*. https://www.marthastewart.com/how-to-build-an-herb-spiral-8672578
- Eden Green. (n.d.). *Hydroponics vs aeroponics: Key differences explained*. https://www.edengreen.com/blog-collection/aeroponics-vs-hydroponics-explained
- Gardeners Basics. (n.d.). *How to grow herbs indoors with grow lights*. https://www.gardenersbasics.com/tools/blog/how-to-grow-herbs-indoors-with-grow-lightssrsltid=AfmBOorvBlfyiEewkz45oqCZHJobi1XTXv-PgNvNySxmncOFPb9eex9az
- GrowVeg. (n.d.). *How to grow new herbs from cuttings*. https://www.growveg.com/guides/how-to-grow-new-herbs-from-cuttings/
- Gardening Know How. (n.d.). *Herb growing problems: Common herb garden pests and solutions*. https://www.gardeningknowhow.com/edible/herbs/hgen/herb-growing-problems.htm
- Garden Therapy. (n.d.). *How to make enough compost for my garden: Urban composting methods*. https://gardentherapy.ca/urban-composting-methods/
- The Herbal Academy. (n.d.). *12 permaculture principles to use when planning your herb garden*. https://theherbalacademy.com/blog/permaculture-principles/
- Garden Punch List. (2017, February). *Herb seeding and growing chart*. https://gardenpunchlist.blogspot.com/2017/02/herb-seeding-and-growing-chart.html
- North Carolina Herb Society. (n.d.). *Herb gardening with climate change*. https://www.ncherbsociety.org/herb-gardening-with-climate-change.html
- Seedtime. (n.d.). *Seedtime—Your ultimate garden planner and management journal*. https://seedtime.us/#:

- Jekka's Herb Farm. (n.d.). *Jekka's top 8 sustainable herb gardening tips.* https://www.jekkas.com/blogs/jekkas-blog/top-sustainable-and-organic-herb-gardening-tipssrsltid=AfmBOoqgj1R8nT4RgpnUmcnIKu8ta_t0ddEj-BwBRx3vqb53fg_XXtgXk

AUTHOR BIO

Kent Jameson grew up in a quaint farm town in Iowa, where he developed a deep appreciation for the simplicity of rural life. In 1994, he earned a Bachelor of Science degree in Family and Consumer Sciences Journalism from Iowa State University, laying the foundation for a life dedicated to exploring the intersection of family, health, and everyday issues that confront people.

Passionate about natural health, alternative medicines, and sustainable living, Kent's writing focuses on issues that directly affect families and consumers, offering thoughtful insights into how people can live healthier, more balanced lives in today's fast-paced world. Whether he's exploring the benefits of organic gardening, promoting holistic wellness practices, or discussing the challenges of modern life, Kent's work is always grounded in practical, real-world experience.

When he's not writing or tending to his garden, Kent enjoys spending time with his two sons, often cheering them on from the sidelines as they play basketball. Currently residing in Phoenix, Arizona, he continues to live by the values of simplicity and wellness that have guided him throughout his life and career.

Made in the USA
Las Vegas, NV
11 April 2025

9ae1b687-cae8-496a-9497-f52f8b3b91aeR01